ALLIED DUNBAR

MONEY GUIDES

YOUR HOME IN SPAIN

Second Edition

YOUR HOME IN SPAIN

PER SVENSSON

Second Edition

Longman

© Allied Dunbar Financial Services Limited 1989

ISBN 0–85121–563–7

Published by

Longman Professional and Business Communications Division
Longman Group UK Limited
21–27 Lamb's Conduit Street, London WC1N 3NJ

Associated Offices

Australia   Longman Professional Publishing (Pty) Limited
130 Phillip Street, Sydney, NSW 2000

Hong Kong   Longman Group (Far East) Limited
Cornwall House, 18th Floor, Taikoo Trading Estate,
Tong Chong Street, Quarry Bay

Malaysia   Longman Malaysia Sdn Bhd
No 3 Jalan Kilang A, Off Jalan Penchala,
Petaling Jaya, Selangor, Malaysia

Singapore   Longman Singapore Publishers (Pte) Ltd
25 First Lok Yang Road, Singapore 2262

USA   Longman Group (USA) Inc
500 North Dearborn Street, Chicago, Illinois 60610

No responsibility for loss occasioned to any person acting or refraining from action as a result of the material in this publication can be accepted by the authors or publishers.

The views and opinions of Allied Dunbar may not necessarily coincide with some of the views and opinions expressed in this book which are solely those of the authors and no endorsement of them by Allied Dunbar should be inferred.

A CIP catalogue record for this book is available from the British Library.

Printed and bound in Great Britain by Mackays of Chatham PLC, Chatham, Kent

Every care has been taken in preparing this book. The guidance it contains is sound at the time of publication but it is not intended to be a substitute for skilled professional assistance except in the most straightforward situations. You are also advised that the law in Spain can and does change quite frequently and it would not be unusual to find individual variations in the different provinces and municipalities.

Because of this, the author, the publishers and Allied Dunbar Financial Services Ltd (or any other company within the Allied Dunbar Group) can take no responsibility for the outcome of action taken or not taken as a result of reading this book.

Preface

As this book was just about to go to print, there was some comment in the British media about the implications of the new coastal law, *La Ley De Costas* (referred to on page 38). It all revolved around what amounted to a misunderstanding of the intentions of the Spanish planning authorities. The new law is an attempt to preserve the Spanish coastline. In brief, there is to be no new development within 100 metres of the coastline and restrictions on developments within 500 metres. They are, in effect, declaring their coastline an 'area of outstanding natural beauty' and controlling all further development in much the same way as happens in the United Kingdom.

A problem they have is with existing development within 100 metres of the beach. On the one hand they wish to preserve the rights of property owners but on the other they do not wish to extend the right to have property on this land indefinitely. They are therefore searching for a formula that will protect the current landowners where property exists but to ensure that the law can be applied as intended at an appropriate time in the future to prevent continuous re-development.

With the illegal property, they are much less sympathetic and take the view that if the building did not have planning permission in the first place then the property owner has nobody to blame but himself. In certain isolated cases (for example, where buildings are built on the beach itself) buildings **could** be demolished. However, in these cases the authorities will merely be exercising similar powers to those enjoyed by planning authorities in the United Kingdom; so the moral is the same — follow the rules.

Parliamentary Office
European Parliament
Rue Belliard
Brussels 1040
Belgium

It is very pleasant to be able to welcome the publication of the latest edition of 'Your Home in Spain'.

During the last four years, I have been continuing my campaign of ensuring that foreigners buying property elsewhere in Europe can do so without the fear of fraud. My experience is that the problems are still there; each day brings its share of letters from people who have experienced difficulties.

For six years now, the Institute of Foreign Property Owners has helped an increasing number of people avoid these problems and this book is a distillation of their experience. Is is only too easy to be carried away in the heat of the moment and undertake a purchase that, with the benefit of hindsight, was hasty and ill-judged. I see the worst excesses of the property market but even where everything is perfectly legal and above board there are still procedures to be followed and laws to be obeyed. Property purchase is rarely straightforward.

The Institute is there to help you make an assessment of the problems that exist and careful reading of this book will prepare you for the sort of things to look out for. I hope the Institute will continue with their work of providing protection to more and more consumers throughout Europe.

Edward McMillan Scott MEP

Per Svensson

The author, Per Svensson, is a Norwegian who was active in Spanish property development from 1966–1980. After a brief retirement, he returned to Spain to found the *Instituto de Propietarios Extranjeros* (Institute of Foreign Property Owners) in Spain.

The Institute is active in all the tourist zones of Spain, giving the foreign property owner information and assistance in a wide range of areas.

The Institute is represented throughout Europe by a number of delegates and administrators and the magazine '*Spain Today*' is published in a number of languages.

Acknowledgements

There is no substitute for knowledge – and in Spain it is important to keep that knowledge up-to-date. Even as we were working on the final manuscript of this edition of 'Your Home in Spain', new laws on local taxes were announced. Some of these will come into effect at the end of 1989; some of them will come into effect the following year. All the changes will affect the foreign property owner.

This book is based on the experiences of thousands of foreign property buyers and owners from all parts of Spain and throughout Europe, often transmitted to us by local delegates or foreign representatives.

Many of the experiences have come from British buyers or owners in Spain. I would also like to acknowledge with gratitude the work done by David Vessey and his colleagues at Allied Dunbar on the manuscript.

Per Svensson
President

Instituto de Propietarios Extranjeros
Avenida de Ifach 1
Edificio El Portal, Apartado 35
Calpe Alicante
346–583–18–97

Contents

8 Paying for your property

Foreword

The number of foreigners who have a property in Spain runs into millions – a group of consumers big enough to be taken seriously by any authority. The total foreign investment resulting from their purchase and subsequent running costs amounts to billions of *pesetas* – a sum sufficient for any Minister of Finance to take careful note.

With the work of the *Instituto de Propietarios Extranjeros* (Institute of Foreign Property Owners) over the years, the foreign property owners and the Spanish authorities have come to realise that the settlement of foreigners on the Spanish coasts and islands is not a passing phenomenon, but something that will continue and grow. We expect the number of foreign property owners in Spain to double before the year 2000.

By then the process of buying a property across the borders in Europe must be made simpler and safer. The buyers must be better informed, and the vendors and builders must accept certain standards.

In addition, the communications between the foreign property owners and residents and the Spanish administration must be improved. As we come increasingly closer to the planned ' citizens' Europe ', the Europeans settling in Spain must not be regarded as 'foreigners' anymore, but as Europeans among Europeans.

The Institute of Foreign Property Owners has grown in a few years to an important organisation of more than 20,000 members. The growth will continue. This is the best guarantee for anyone contemplating buying a property in Spain.

1 Introduction

If you've bought a property in Spain or are considering doing so, then you're not alone. In the last 30 years or so more than one million people have acquired property along the Spanish Mediterranean coast or on the islands. One million properties used by an average of three people per property means three million foreigners either living permanently or for part of the year in Spain.

It is migration that has taken place and is still taking place. The door opener, of course, was mass tourism, making the people from northern Europe more aware of the warmer and sunnier parts of the European continent. Now, with higher living standards and longer holidays, it's a new phase in the development of the affluent society. After buying a house with a fridge, freezer, dishwasher, stereo, video, compact disc player, a second car and all the other necessities of life, a home in southern Europe is, for many people, the ultimate luxury.

The British move in

The Germans must take the credit for starting the trend as they were the first to see the advantages of the Mediterranean coastline compared with their cold winters and wet summers. For many years, the British found it difficult to buy property abroad due to exchange control but since these restrictions were lifted, British buyers have taken the lead.

To date, no other nation has bought so many properties as the British and they have flocked to join the Germans, people from the Scandinavian countries and the rest of Europe. Now even the Americans and the Japanese are buying thereby adding to the more than 30 different nationalities that you can find on the Spanish Mediterranean coastline.

What this book is all about

The purpose of this book is to explain the ways in which you can go about buying a home in Spain and settling there, and it will also cover some of the problems that you might come up against along the way. It's not that buying property in Spain is difficult – but it is different and there's a tendency for people buying property abroad to pretend that the differences aren't there. It's very easy when you're on holiday in Spain, surrounded by people from Britain and being looked after by friendly English-speaking hotel staff, to imagine that part of the UK has mysteriously been transported to the Spanish coastline. Buying property in Spain may appear to be little different from buying property in England when you are having it explained to you in a seminar in Tunbridge Wells.

However, if you are buying a home in Spain, the reality is:

- You are buying a home in a foreign country.
- The contract may be in a foreign language.
- The legal system is totally different.
- Spain still has exchange control.
- Spain has a different tax system.

Provided you follow the rules, you will have no problems. But in order to follow the rules properly, you must be prepared to pay for expert advice and help. Why omit to do things that you wouldn't dream of forgetting to do if you were buying a home in the UK? Here, you expect to pay a solicitor to ensure that all the legalities are tied up – but some people still buy homes in Spain without a thought for the legal niceties. It would be beyond belief – if it didn't happen.

Be prepared to get advice

So, if you're thinking of buying – do look for some sensible advice. You've taken the first step by buying this book – there are other sources of help available to you which will make sure that buying your home in Spain will be straightforward and painless. The Institute of Foreign Property Owners was set up to help people from all over Europe with property purchase in Spain and this book is structured very largely on their knowledge and experience.

Assistance is available to individual members from the Institute's central administration and from local delegates and co-ordinators based in all the tourist zones and in other countries. Through its members' magazine, members of the Institute are kept up-to-date with information – the key word for the property purchaser and owner in Spain. We expect to keep in touch with matters affecting our homes in the UK usually by reading the national and local newspapers. Most of us can't do this in Spain – but it doesn't make it any less important to keep up-to-date with developments as they affect what could well be a substantial financial investment.

Some of the problem areas

Many people from Britain have come to Spain with great hopes and have seen those hopes realised. They have bought their home in Spain and for them it has become a source of considerable pleasure. For others – happily, only a small proportion – the reality has been quite different and their dream has been wrecked by lack of preparation and by trying to speed the process up by cutting corners.

In some cases, this has been the result of deliberate fraud – and this, it has to be said, is not necessarily as a result of 'over enthusiasm' at the Spanish end. Regrettably, a small number of Britons have seen overseas property purchase as an excellent way of relieving their fellow countrymen of their wealth. It's very easy to disguise fraud when you are surrounded with papers written in a foreign language – but that can be even more reason for getting expert help.

Consumer protection

The Spanish Government have been sufficiently alert to this problem and recently extended the laws of consumer protection to include property purchase. The new law contains a range of measures to make sure that consumers are protected from bad contracts and poor workmanship. But, like all other laws, they are designed to provide a framework under which you can exercise your rights but are only designed to actually trap the worst excesses. Marginal cases are unlikely ever to get to official light and in any case, your best protection is your own care and foresight.

This book is not meant to be anecdotal but here is one small story to illustrate just how extreme the problem can be. The Institute of Foreign Property Owners were approached by an Englishman who announced his intention of buying a bar in Benidorm. The Institute were more than willing to help and their first question was 'can you speak Spanish?'. The reply was that it wasn't necessary for him to speak Spanish because he would only be serving behind the bar. Not only had he no clue at all as to the concept of setting up and opening a business in Spain, he appeared to have little idea of what running a bar entailed!

The seizure of property

Every now and again, a particular horror story of life in Spain hits the headlines in this country but by digging beneath the surface, it's often the case that the error is the result of poor preparation or total misunderstanding of the way things happen in Spain. One popular misunderstanding (and one which occasionally attracts widespread headlines) is the seizure of property by the Spanish authorities. When it happens, the natural question to ask is – 'could it happen to me?' The simple answer is – 'yes' – but things have to get to a pretty bad state for seizure of property to actually happen.

The Spanish authorities are no different from those of any other country. They make laws and impose taxes, at both local and national level. Where they differ from the UK authorities is that they place much more reliance on the individual finding out what taxes he should pay and by when. The authorities, of course, know how much tax they are owed – it's just that they seem rather reluctant to write to you if you forget.

Consequently, a debt can be registered against you and if you don't pay, then you are fined. They don't necessarily tell you about that either – they just add the fine to the debt. As time goes by and the debt mounts up, the authorities look for ways of recovering the debt – and the simplest solution is to seize whatever of your assets they can get hold of. For most Britons, this means their property and so the way is open to the authorities to seize that and sell it – which **occasionally** they do.

The early warning system

But you do have the means of protecting yourself because the names of debtors are published in official bulletins. Consequently, you get an 'early warning' if you are one of the many thousands of people throughout Spain who inadvertently run up a small official debt. One of the services that the Institute of Foreign Property Owners provides, is to reproduce the lists for the tourist regions in its magazine and, if you ask, to investigate the reasons why your name appears there.

Once again, it's information that provides the answer and hopefully this book will provide you with much more. It looks at all the various matters you should bear in mind when looking at property in Spain and covers in some detail the steps that you should take to ensure that ownership of your new home is legally secure and that you have paid for it in the correct way.

You can then do what you set out to do – enjoy your new Spanish home in the way that the rest of us do.

2 Where to buy

Geography of Spain

Spain is the second most mountainous country in Europe, second only to Switzerland. The amount of significant flat land is therefore very limited and tends to be concentrated on the coastal strip alongside the Mediterranean (apart, of course, from the high plains – the *Meseta* – that dominate the centre of Spain).

It is the mountains that play a major part in the climate of Spain. Whilst most people think of Spain as a hot, dry country, it has, in fact, a very varied climate. Madrid, for example, suffers from extremes of temperature with hot summers and freezing winters whereas in the north on the Atlantic coast, the climate will be very familiar to the visitor from Britain.

However, most people looking for a home in Spain are drawn to the Mediterranean coast. It is here that they get what they want – warmth – and it is here that they experience the true Mediterranean climate – hot, dry summers and warm, wet (but not too wet) winters.

The three main coastal areas are Catalonia at the northern end (principally the Costa Brava), Andalusia at the southern end (the Costa del Sol and Costa de la Luz) and Valencia in the middle (the Costa Blanca) with Murcia squeezed in between Valencia and Andalusia.

For those who prefer the island life there are the Balearic

Islands (Majorca, Ibiza and Menorca) in the Mediterranean and the Canaries (Gran Canaria, Tenerife and Lanzarote) in the Atlantic, off the African coast.

The climate

The climate in the Mediterranean area is remarkably consistent in all the coastal areas. In summer, the average minimum temperature will rarely dip below 65° Fahrenheit and will usually be up in the mid 80s at the hottest time of the day. In winter, of course, it is cooler. It will usually be around 60° on average at its warmest but will rarely dip below the low 40s (though the Costa del Sol does have warmer winters than elsewhere).

For real winter warmth you will have to go to the Canaries. There you can expect it to be in the 70s and only to fall to the 60° Fahrenheit mark at the cooler times of the day.

The one thing that Spain does seem to bring to the climate is a lack of extremes. Although it can get hot, it is never too hot and although you can get a number of chilly days, it is rare to find frost on the coast (although Majorca can claim to have had some heavy snowfalls, much to the surprise of the inhabitants). It is this lack of extremes which led Javea on the Costa Blanca, north of Alicante, to be chosen by the World Health Organisation as having the most acceptable climate to the average Western European. It was chosen on the basis of this overall average – it is never too hot and it is never too cold, it is never too humid and it is never too dry.

How to get there

Spain has virtually led the way in low-priced holidays and
that has led to the development of a very good charter flight
business between the UK and Spain. It is now possible to fly
from every major airport in the UK and virtually every area
that you would consider for buying property in Spain is within
easy reach of an airport. There are airports on the three
Balearic Islands and also on the islands in the Canaries. On
the Mediterranean coastline, (and going from north to
south), there are airports at:

— Gerona
— Barcelona
— Reus
— Tarragona
— Valencia
— Alicante
— San Javier, Murcia
— Almeria
— Malaga.

And for those going even further south, there is always the
airport at Gibraltar.

In addition, for those who want to travel by car, the Spanish
road system is designed for fast travel. Although the coastal
motorway doesn't extend all the way down to the Costa del
Sol, it is now possible to travel at high speed all the way
from the Channel ports as far as Alicante with only one small
break in the route round Valencia.

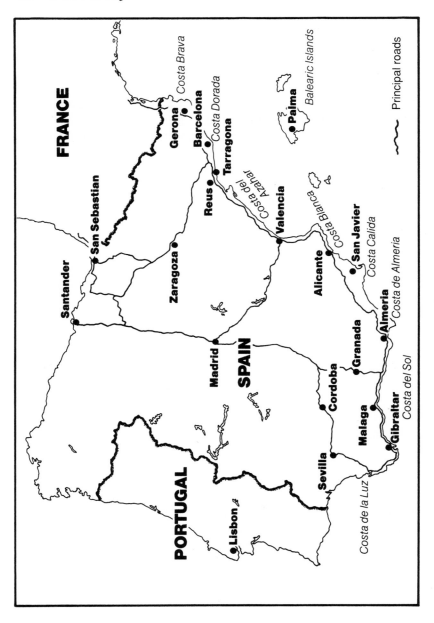

Where should you buy?

Clearly, there will be parts of Spain that you are familiar with but there may also be some areas that you hadn't previously thought of that might be worth a visit. The whole of the Mediterranean coastline is, in fact, divided up into a series of 'Costas' some of them familiar and some of them not so familiar.

At the top, is the **Costa Brava**, the 'wild coast'. As its name suggests, this is an area of cliffs, sheltered coves, hills and valleys. On the coast, you will find that many urbanisations have grown up. Worth considering is the Bay of Rosas (just south of the French border) with the towns of Rosas and La Escala with the huge yacht harbour development of Ampuriabrava.

Further south is Estartit with its yacht harbour and miles of beaches and beyond that you will find the harbour town of Palamos and San Antonio de Calonge with good beaches and a range of building developments. Well-known by the holiday makers are San Feliu, Tossa, Lloret de Mar and, right at the southern end of the coast, Blanes.

The **Costa Dorada**, the 'golden coast', stretches from Blanes to the mouth of the River Ebro. Overall, the coastal area is flatter than the Costa Brava, but inland the mountains start climbing once again.

The coastline incorporates the major towns of Barcelona and Tarragona but the main property areas start south of Barcelona at the town of Sitges with its miles of beaches. This town has grown rapidly since it was 'discovered' in the early 1960s and now has a cosmopolitan touch. Further south come Villanueva, Comarruga, with its beaches and the fishing village of Torredembarra.

South of Tarragona are Salou and Cambrils and, right at the

end of the Costa Dorada, where the River Ebro meets the Mediterranean, lies San Carlos de Rapita with its very extensive quiet beaches.

Beyond the River Ebro is the **Costa del Azahar**, the 'coast of the orange flower'. This is even less well-known among foreign property owners. It is the coastline from the River Ebro to Denia and includes the provinces of Castellon and Valencia. There are a number of popular resorts on this coast, among them Peniscola and Gandia and the amount of available property is increasing quite rapidly. However, the gulf of Valencia incorporates a number of industrial towns and so there are parts of the Costa del Azahar which suffer from industrial pollution.

From Denia to the Mar Menor, lies the **Costa Blanca**, the 'white coast', one of the most popular areas of Spain, both for tourism and property. And it is not just the coastline that is popular. Very many houses have been built in places like Pego and Orba which are many miles inland. This is not surprising because the inland valleys of the province of Alicante are very attractive with towns such as Callosa de Ensarria, Tarbena, and Parcent. Many people have built properties in the Jalon valley one of the most extensive agricultural areas on the whole of the coast. On the coast itself are Denia (with its wide beaches, ferry connections to Ibiza and many urbanisations) and Javea, both very popular with the foreign property buyer.

Just around the corner is Moraira rapidly emerging as a holiday town with new hotels and a marina. There is good property here in the valleys and nearby bays.

Close by is Calpe sheltering under the Penon de Ifach, one of the most famous landmarks on the Costa Blanca, followed by Altea, one of the most ancient towns on the Costa Blanca which is more residential than tourist and so has been able to preserve its character. Further south of course is Benidorm, the capital of the Costa Blanca. Benidorm has one of the most extensive beaches in Europe and, if you look hard enough, you can still find the old village. However, do bear in mind that 8% of Europe's charter tourism comes here so don't expect year round peace and tranquillity. Close to Benidorm is Villajoyosa which is an older town but where urbanisations are slowly making their presence felt.

Alicante itself has very little beach but just at the south of it (and very close to the international airport) there are long stretches of good beaches and sand dunes. Santa Pola and Guardamar are becoming more popular and further south, Torrevieja and Cabo Roig are very popular with the second home owner.

After Costa Blanca, comes the **Costa Calida**, the 'hot coast', which stretches the short distance from the Mar Menor in the north to Aguilas in the south.

The Mar Menor is unique. It is a large area of shallow sea separated from the rest of the Mediterranean by a narrow strip of sand. On this strip there are many properties and the area of water which is sheltered by the sand strip has made the Mar Menor an all year round attraction for windsurfers and dinghy sailers. It also has an 18 hole golf course, at the high class urbanisation of Club la Manga.

Beyond the Mar Menor there are good beaches and areas that are relatively undeveloped.

The **Costa de Almeria** (the Almerian coast) begins just beyond Aguilas and is one of the most untouched areas as far as foreign property buyers are concerned. There are a number of small settlements here most of which are virtually undiscovered. Indeed, on the entire Mediterranean coastline, Almeria is the province least touched by industry and tourism and where you can still find places at prices that have been unknown for years on other parts of the coast. Of course, Almeria also has some well-known places; Mojacar, Aguadulce, Roquetas de Mar and Almerimar are popular with tourist and property buyer alike.

After Almeria comes the **Costa del Sol**, the 'sun coast'. Along
with the Costa Blanca, the Costa del Sol is an immensely
popular area with the British property owner. It stretches all
the way to Gibraltar where the Mediterranean meets the
Atlantic Ocean. As with the Costa Blanca, many people have
bought properties inland. The Sierra Nevada is one of the
most popular mountain areas in Spain and many people have
bought farmhouses in the valleys on its southern slopes.

On the coast, Nerja is the real boom town in this region. It
has a well preserved old town but it is beginning to see the
development of a number of urbanisations and apartments.
On the other side of Malaga, Torremolinos was once the
leading place for foreign tourism and settlement on the Costa
del Sol. Not any more though, because, while it is close to
the airport, it is probably a little too close and it is beginning
to merge with the city of Malaga itself.

From Torremolinos to Gibraltar you will find hundreds of
urbanisations, building projects and developments, mostly
catering for the foreign property buyer. The development
goes well inland; the villages of Benalmadena and Mijas have
now been taken over by tourism – but by no means destroyed.
The old ways of doing things are still very much in evidence
and many of the old values have been preserved.

Fuengirola has grown in a few years from a small fishing
village to a big town, with an impressive promenade along
the beach. Further south is Marbella which is world famous
as a place of 'beautiful' people with a somewhat 'hot'
nightlife, centred around the yacht harbour of Puerto Banus.
Marbella still has an old town which, as with Benidorm,
many people miss completely because they don't know it
exists.

Estepona also has a charming old town. There are many
urbanisations for foreigners but less tourism. Manilva is
becoming increasingly popular with its vineyards and its new
yacht harbour and beyond Manilva is the urbanisation of
Sotogrande which is particularly well planned and maintained.

Finally, at the end of the Costa del Sol is Gibraltar.

Then comes the **Costa de la Luz** the 'coast of light'. This is the stretch of coast from Gibraltar to the Portuguese border and for most foreign property purchasers it remains unknown territory. Tourists often miss it but it has beautiful beaches, washed by the Atlantic and a temperate climate. Worth considering are Atlanterra, with one of the best beaches in Spain, Playa de Barrosa, Chipionia and Sanlucar de Barrameda. Beaches on either side of Huelva are excellent but, once again, relatively unknown. Inland from the Costa de la Luz are some of the most famous towns in Spain. Sevilla is a remarkable place to visit and so is Jerez de la Frontera, the centre of the sherry producing areas.

The **Balearic Islands** are becoming increasingly popular with the foreign property buyer. Majorca is the main area and although it suffers in summer from a significant amount of tourist traffic, you can still be close to the beaches and well away from the package tours. Majorca is very varied with many surprising and picturesque places so you can always find a good spot for settling down. Wherever it is, you'll always be close to the capital, close to the beaches and close to the airport. Ibiza too is a place where you can find good quality property and yet still be away from the tourist areas but Menorca is much more peaceful, with much less tourism and a good place to consider if you are an 'island man'.

If you want to make absolutely sure of warm weather throughout the winter, then it's the **Canary Islands**. Gran Canaria has the most tourism with the capital, Las Palmas at the southern end of the island having the greatest concentration of tourist hotels.

Tenerife is famous for its volcanic Teide with most urbanisations centred around Puerto de la Cruz but the area in the south including Playa de las Americas is becoming increasingly popular after the opening of a new international airport in the south of the island.

Finally, Lanzarote (and to a lesser extent Fuertaventura) are both volcanic islands of quite outstanding attraction. The climate here is one where it almost never rains and this is leading to a significant amount of property building as the sun seekers from the north move in.

Overall, the Canary Islands are not as inexpensive as they used to be. The demand for property is growing all the time and prices are rapidly moving up to equal (and in some cases overtake) prices on the mainland.

3 What to do and what not to do

The British tend to like Spain, particularly the coastal areas – and the Spanish on the coasts tend to like the British. They are not **too** enthusiastic about the 'lager-louts' who descend on the main tourist towns in July and August, but they are very tolerant even towards them.

And why not? Foreigners have contributed in many ways to the Spanish way of life over the years (a Briton virtually built the port of Denia on the Costa Blanca) and tourism has helped the coastal areas to obtain their affluence.

But they also think the British are a little odd. A popular saying on the Costa Blanca is 'the British leave their brains behind at Alicante Airport'. A little unkind, perhaps, but it is due to the unholy mess that some of us get ourselves into when buying property.

This chapter, then, is a quick, easy-to-read guide to some of the things you should think about when you're buying property in Spain. There is nothing particularly magical about any of it. Buying property anywhere can be a hassle at the best of times (it's reckoned to be one of the most stressful activities you can take part in) but, for some reason, we seem to expect it to be trouble free in Spain just because the sun shines.

Remember, if you were buying property in the UK, you would probably go about it as follows:

● You wouldn't necessarily buy the first house you saw and you certainly wouldn't sign any kind of agreement there and then.

- You would work out what you could afford and you would be careful not to over commit yourself.
- You would want to make absolutely certain that your solicitor had done his job properly and that there were no legal or planning permission problems undiscovered.
- You would get the financial position sorted out before you signed the contract and committed yourself to the purchase.
- If the house you were buying was a second home, you would make yourself familiar with the tax position on owning property in addition to your 'main residence'.
- When you were sure that the house was what you wanted, within your reach, legally problem free and that you had the money to buy the house, then you would go ahead.

Buying property, in Spain, is no different. It's just that people think that it's different and are prepared to do far more on trust.

The majority of builders in the UK are decent, honest businessmen. But would you **really** trust a builder, or a developer, or an estate agent, to undertake all the necessary legal work on your behalf? Most people wouldn't – until they come to Spain and then for some reason, they think that the rules are different.

This chapter is written for you.

Watch your budget

- Don't over commit yourself. If you feel £35,000 is the most you can afford, go for a property costing £33,000 as a cushion against worsening exchange rates. Don't bank on exchange rates getting better – just regard it as a bonus if they do.
- Knock at least 10% off your limit and put that on one side for legal and other costs. It's better to know that

your purchase is all above board rather than to have a better range of fitted units in the kitchen. Also, you will have taxes and fees to pay when you buy your property and these can be quite high.

- Budget your running costs and then only buy property that you can easily afford to maintain (and remember you have taxes and rates to pay as well). Don't forget, you get paid in the UK in sterling and you have to cope with inflation. On top of that, you now have to face a fluctuating exchange rate and Spanish inflation as well.

Look before you buy

- There is a temptation to make up your mind on the first visit. But it isn't that difficult to make a return trip under your own steam and that would give you a chance to really look at things properly.
- Don't make up your mind in Spain – make your decisions back home. It's a major decision – don't rush it.
- When you go on your first visit, take a camera and plenty of film. You may not get another chance to remind yourself of everything you've seen – photographs will help.
- If you are looking for a timeshare, make sure you are dealing with a reputable company – a member of the Timeshare Developers Association would be a good starting point.
- Don't be hassled into buying. It's a buyer's market and the agents and developers need you more than you need them.
- Don't sign anything when you first meet the builder or developer. If you like the look of a particular property, make sure you return to the United Kingdom with:
  — a plan of the property.
  — a plan of the area showing where the property is to be built.

- a full specification (ie the materials with which the property is to be built).
- a full list of the fixtures and fittings.
- a copy of the contract, in English.
- If you feel under pressure to sign some kind of 'intention to buy' make sure that you only sign a non-binding reservation, not an option where the final purchasing terms are not clearly and completely spelled out.

The legal side

- Do engage the services of a Spanish lawyer and make sure you instruct him carefully. He will do as you wish but do ask for evidence that he has done it. Don't assume that it's all been done for you – get it in writing.
- Don't sign anything unless you have discussed it with your lawyer first.
- Never pay over any money unless your lawyer tells you it is in order.
- Open your Spanish bank account early (you can do it from the UK) and make sure that your payments for your property are backed-up by a 'bank certificate'. This will be done by your bank if you ask them and, when your house is finished, they will also ensure that all your regular bills are paid by standing order so that you can then forget them.

Dealing with the developer

Don't sign a purchase contract that doesn't cover the special needs of Spain – the following points are to guide you towards some specific problem areas that your lawyer can check:

- It should clearly indicate whether the seller is also the owner of the property, a registered real estate agent or has power of attorney from the owner.
- The contract should specify that the building project or urbanisation has been approved by the authorities.
- It should **explicitly** state that there are no outstanding debts on the property or land.
- It should guarantee that you will get the title deeds and all other necessary documents **at the same time** as you pay the final payment towards the purchase.
- It should allow you to withhold at least 10% for up to six months as a guarantee against the builder not correcting faults in the property.
- It should confirm which services are to be connected to your property on completion (eg water, electricity, roads).
- It should not oblige you to pay in a way that gets round Spain's foreign currency regulations.
- If you are paying for your home by instalments, make sure you pay only when the builder completes each stage. Never sign anything which commits you to payments on a fixed schedule. Your builder may be late – why should you be early?
- If you are buying on plans before the dwelling is finished, you have a legal right to get a guarantee for your payments, through a bank or an insurance company. You also have the legal right to get a guarantee for your payments (through a bank or an insurance company) which will ensure that your money is refunded if the builder, for whatever reason, is unable to finish the construction.
- It should not require you to pay money to the agent or to anybody other than the person from whom you are going to buy the property.

The list seems rather daunting – but there is nothing particularly unusual in it to anybody familiar with buying a house in the UK. As we said at the beginning, buying property in Spain is no different – it's just that people think it's different.

A last word on tax. Make sure you pay all your taxes when you buy your property and make sure you pay all your annual taxes on time. If you ignore this, you are building up problems for the future. It's very simple to appoint somebody to do it on your behalf.

You may meet people who tell you that Spain is a tax haven because nobody bothers to check up on you. Putting a false value in the deeds of your house is 'the Spanish way of doing things' they will tell you. You are strongly advised to ignore all this kind of 'expert' advice. It may have been true in the past – it is most certainly not true today. The Spanish tax authorities are rapidly catching up on all kinds of tax evasion and you may find that bending the rules today will earn you a hefty tax bill tomorrow.

4 What to buy

Introduction

By and large, there are two main ways of buying property in
Spain:

1   You can do it the easy way and buy an existing house or
    apartment (either a second-hand house or a new one) or
    buy one that is going to be built in an existing
    development.
2   If you are more adventurous, you can buy a plot of land
    and get a builder to construct one for you.

This chapter will look at how you can go about searching for
property with some thoughts on second-hand houses. It also
covers the rules for buying subsidised houses. If you decide
you would prefer a new house (either completed or in course
of construction) or if you wish to buy a plot of land, you will
find full details in chapters 5 and 6.

Not so very long ago, most people looking for a home in
Spain started by buying a plot and putting their individual
dream house on it. As land prices and construction costs have
soared, this particular approach has become more and more
difficult for most property buyers. Also, the maintenance costs
of larger properties have increased considerably and this is an
important consideration when you are looking around for any
property.

The result is that most people are now buying either
apartments or pueblo-style houses. There's a good deal of

sense in this but you must remember that if you buy a unit in a group, you are buying something else as well – you will be buying the responsibilities of being one of a community and there will be the regular community charges to think about (you will find more information about living in a community in chapter 14).

What you decide to buy will obviously depend very much on how you intend using the property and whether you will be using it only for holidays or for more permanent residence. It will depend on the size of your family, your sporting and cultural interests, whether you like sailing and other sea based activities and, inevitably, the amount of money you can afford to spend. Apartments, terraced houses, semi-detached houses with a small plot, village properties with larger plots and building land are all readily available.

Think about selling

The other point you must bear in mind, before you buy, is what you will do when you want to sell your property. Whatever the reasons may be, it will then be very important that the property fits not only your individual tastes and needs but that it has general appeal as well. There has been a buyer's market for the last few years, with many more resale properties on offer than there have been buyers. At the same time, the number of new properties on the market is growing all the time and so it may not necessarily be very straightforward to resell your property in the future. Some types of property, of course, and also some areas, are in such high demand that you get local sellers' markets and you will have no difficulty in selling your property at any time. Nevertheless, it is an important consideration and so you should be looking for your new property from a number of different points of view.

If you intend to stay in Spain for any length of time, it might pay you to buy a small property to start with, (and one that can be easily resold), until you are quite sure that Spain is the place for you. This will also give you the opportunity to become acquainted with a particular area and will give you the opportunity, of course, to find your final 'dream house'. Some people are even more cautious and start by renting a property for a period, using it as a base for further investigations before committing any capital. This can often be a sensible approach – and inexpensive if you rent outside the main holiday seasons.

How to find the property

There are two basic ways to start looking for a property in Spain. On the one hand, you can look at the advertisements that you will find in many national newspapers in the UK. On the other hand, you can come to Spain and find a suitable property or sales organisation yourself.

The simplest way, of course, is to start by reading the advertisements in your national newspapers and send for information on those which appear to be the most interesting. As you gradually find out more about the various companies operating in the field, you will find the ones which seem well established but do make sure to pick up information from more than one company so that you can compare prices and offers.

From time to time, you will find that a number of property companies arrange seminars and exhibitions, often in local hotels. If you can get along to see one of these, it would be a very good opportunity to see first-hand the sort of properties being offered. Once again, by comparing two or three such exhibitions, you will gradually get an idea of those people who really do know what they're talking about and those who have got good opportunities to offer you.

You will find that the people promoting Spanish property in the UK fall into three categories:

1   Independent agents who may represent a range of builders or developers in Spain (and any one developer may negotiate terms with a range of independent agents).
2   Estate agents in this country who have expanded into Europe and provide a similar service to that which they provide in the UK.
3   Spanish developers themselves who have set up sales outlets in the UK and promote their own properties on their own behalf.

Seeing for yourself

Sooner or later, though, you are going to have to take the plunge and go out to Spain and see for yourself. It's no good relying on memories of a two week holiday on which to base your decision on where to live in Spain. You have got to go out and see for yourself and preferably at a time when it might not be looking at its most glamorous. You will find that many developers will lay on long weekends (Thursday to Sunday is a popular timescale) and some of them will offer you the opportunity to travel free and also put you up in a hotel at their expense. On the other hand, the only properties you are going to see by this route are those that the developer has on offer but it can be an inexpensive way of seeing a particular area. Some developers aren't quite this generous; they make **you** pay, with the incentive that they will refund the costs if you sign on the dotted line. On balance, it's probably better to pay the bill and sign on the dotted line when it suits you, not the developer.

Arranging a visit yourself

These long weekends are a good opportunity to have a look around but why not be a little more courageous and make the trip under your own steam? If you are thinking of spending many thousands of pounds on a property in Spain, it really does make a lot of sense to spend some time looking at all the opportunities open to you. It is, of course, very straightforward to do this – any travel agent will be able to fix you up with a charter flight, inexpensive hotel accommodation and a hire car and you will find that rates in the autumn and winter are not at all expensive.

Do take the time to look around properly. If you are going to move into an area you will need to know as much about it as you would about a new area in the UK. The one thing that most popular areas in Spain aren't short of is fellow countrymen. You can always find somebody to talk to in a restaurant or bar who will be more than pleased to give you as much information as you are likely to be able to absorb in a week!

Finding the seller

In Spain, only three categories of people can lawfully organise a sale of property:

1   The owner of the property.
2   Someone who has the owner's power of attorney to do so.
3   A registered real estate agent.

In practice, this does not present much of a problem to the buyer. Although you won't find as many estate agents in the Spanish high street as you will at home, there are a number of organisations that will be offering property for sale (both new and second-hand) and most of them will always have somebody who can speak English. If you have taken the trouble to go to Spain and look for yourself, it can be very worthwhile just wandering up and down the main street of the local town looking for the *agente de propiedad* and doing exactly what you do in England – ie compare prices.

Buying second-hand property

You will find a reasonable amount of second-hand property on sale, some of it advertised in the national newspapers at home and some of it, of course, for sale in the estate agents. Some of it may often have an attractive price if it turns out that the owner is forced to sell it for some reason or that he himself bought some time ago for a good price. But do bear in mind that old properties may be built with low quality materials and they may lack the stricter degree of control in construction that exists today. Repairing an old house with a problem can be expensive – particularly when you are in a foreign country.

If you are trying to buy second-hand property from the UK, then you will find a number of people advertising in the national newspapers. Alternatively, try and get hold of copies of the local expatriate newspapers from Spain, most of which carry a fair amount of property advertising. Once again, there's no way you will be able to buy the property without going to see it but do make sure you arrange to view a good range of property before making a special trip. If at all possible, try and get the sellers to send you as many photographs as they can of the property. If they are unable to do this, it's worth wondering why.

Things to check with second-hand property

When you are buying second-hand property, you will need to know that the person selling it has got good title to it, ie that he is in a position to sell it. You will need to know the full address of the property, and information about the property and its registration number from the property register (which you will find on the seller's copy of the *escritura*, the title deeds of the property). You should then get your lawyer to write to the property registry to find out if the details on the *escritura* are correct, ie that the seller is the owner of the property and there are no debts on it. You will find full details of this in chapter 7.

In addition to the registration details, you should ask for the last receipts for electricity and water and also the last receipt for the local rates. You should only pay a small deposit on account of the price agreed, pointing out in writing at the time that the sale is on condition that all payments, taxes and charges are kept up-to-date until the day the property is transferred to you.

If you buy a second-hand house, the electricity company have the power to demand that it is re-wired before you get a new contract in your own name so that it conforms with new safety standards. That's something to check out before you buy the property and make quite sure when you move to your new property that the supply contract is re-written in your name. If it remains in the name of the previous owner, you are liable for any debts he may have left.

Finally, check out the position with regard to the taxes that will arise when you buy property, (you will find full details in chapter 10).

All these checks are important to make quite sure that, once having bought the property and paid over the purchase money, there are no nasty surprises waiting for you.

Special rules on subsidised houses

The idea of being able to buy a home at something under the full economic price is always attractive. This is relatively common in Britain where there is council housing and also starter homes. Things are rather different in Spain; local authority housing hardly exists but the corresponding needs of property for people on relatively low incomes is met by what are called *VPOs* (*Viviendas de Proteccion Oficial*) which are officially protected and subsidised dwellings.

VPOs were officially introduced to help lower paid people, but with the growing prosperity of the country, Spanish people themselves were starting to buy *VPOs* as second homes near the coast. As a result rules were introduced to restrict sales of *VPOs* to people who can confirm that they will be living in the property themselves. There is also a second restriction, that only families with a salary of less than five times the minimum general salary are eligible to buy a *VPO*.

The question, of course, is whether as a foreigner it's possible for you to buy one as your principal residence. The Spanish legislation is no different from any other legislation throughout the world – it's difficult to get a straight 'yes' or 'no' as to whether or not foreigners can buy officially subsidised houses.

Nevertheless, it does happen.

The advantages and disadvantages of a *VPO*

The advantages of buying a subsidised house built under a public grant are not only that you are paying a lower price but that you may also get a preferential mortgage and pay relatively low interest rates compared to the open market. Also, during the first three years, you will usually have no capital payments, just interest. In addition, all payments are guaranteed by a recognised public insurance company and the building quality is controlled by the local authorities.

Overall, it can be quite a useful way to get into the housing market in Spain. You are getting a lower mortgage and it is likely that your total initial payments are going to be between 40% and 50% of the total purchasing price (and you should beware of any developers' claims that it would be less than this). In some cases, you could well find that the developer comes up with a slightly different arrangement under the terms of which the subsidised mortgage never materialises and you are committed to a normal mortgage (ie with higher interest payments) which is something you don't want.

If you are offered property that's been built on a grant, you should make doubly sure to check the contract and put a clause in this to say that the promoter is obliged to reimburse all the money and interest paid if you don't obtain the promised mortgage.

Needless to say, there is a snag and, as you might expect with subsidised housing, it concerns your freedom to sell. If you wish to sell the property on the open market, you may have to fulfil the following conditions before you can:

● You must repay to the authorities the outstanding capital on the mortgage.
● You must also pay to the authorities the difference between the original subsidised price and the current open market price.

The property is then re-designated (ie it becomes non-subsidised) and you may then sell it as you wish. After you have been in the property for four years, you may sell without having to fulfil the second condition.

If you are buying subsidised housing as a second-hand house, then you must make sure to find out whether it is still subsidised or whether it has been redesignated. If it has not and you pay a price over and above the valuation for a *VPO*, then you may have trouble finalising the legal details.

5 Buying new property

Introduction

When you buy new property (and this will generally either be in course of construction or to be built from scratch) four basic stages have to be gone through:

1 Planning permission has to be obtained from the local authority.
2 Plans have to be drawn up with an architect.
3 You will need a firm contract with the builder.
4 You need to ensure good legal title to the property when it is finished.

This chapter will concentrate on dealing with the Town Hall and finding your way around the planning rules, together with the things to bear in mind when designing a house to your own specification. Chapter 6 will cover the contractual aspects that should be sorted out with your builder and Chapter 7 explains the legal process you must go through to get good title to your property.

Much of this chapter will deal specifically with building your own house but even if you are buying from a developer you cannot assume that the planning aspects have been correctly dealt with. You should always ask for evidence that the property is being built in accordance with the planning rules – which in Spain are getting tighter all the time.

The planning rules

At one time, building property in Spain was a very casual affair with little attention being paid to local planning rules. That is no longer the case and you'll find that the planning regulations in Spain are as tight as they are in the UK. It's therefore important when considering building property that you make sure that you apply for planning permission and that if you're buying a partially built house, that the builder has obtained planning permission as well.

The problem of planning permission had been building up for some time. Even as recently as November 1987, the local authorities announced an 'amnesty' to over 100 illegal urbanisations (with the warning that they wouldn't be so relaxed in future). And it isn't just the coastal regions, it's a problem which has developed throughout Spain where an increasing number of houses and urbanisations have been built without full planning permission.

The Town Halls are now waking up to the problem. They are realising that badly designed and illegal developments can quickly become substandard and detract from the areas as a whole and so they are now getting much tighter in the way they control building. There's no particular problem in this as far as the property buyer is concerned – it just means that you need to take more care than you might have had to some time ago to make sure that you get permission before starting to build.

In many cases, you will find that where you intend to build is covered by good planning rules and that the person who is building the property is required to follow these rules to the letter. In some cases, the local authority will demand financial guarantees from developers in order to ensure that the final infrastructure of the development is satisfactory eg that the roads are wide enough for traffic, that they are able to withstand the heat and occasional torrential rain, that the water pipes can supply the water that's required in the peak season and that the sewage disposal system works.

In other areas, you may find that the planning regulations aren't quite so tight but that's not a reason for congratulation. You may subsequently find that the planning rules tighten up to the extent that the property owner then becomes responsible for the things which the developer left out. This could range from putting in street lights and pavements to installing adequate electricity substations or sewage disposal systems.

It's therefore important if you're considering building new property to investigate the planning regulations thoroughly and to find out just how tight they are. If they don't seem tight at all, then that may be a good reason for building your property somewhere else.

Buying a newly built property

A newly built property will normally have been built with better materials and under new and stricter building regulations. Naturally, you are not going to get any choice in the finish or in the fixtures and fittings. Also a house that has been built speculatively may be rather more expensive because the developer is going to include in the price the costs of financing the construction and some element of compensation for the risks he is running by building speculatively in the first place.

When you buy a newly built property, it probably won't have been registered for local rates, it probably won't have the certificate of habitability issued and will probably have no electricity and water contracts. You should first find out from the Town Hall that the property has been built in accordance with the local planning rules for the area and that it is connected to all the local services according to the plans from the point of view of roads, water supply, electricity supply and sewage.

In any case, you would be well advised to check with the water company and the electricity company that the services are available and also ask them to confirm in writing that the services will be provided when you or the builder supply them with the necessary documents.

Once you have got all these documents, it is enough to go along to the Town Hall and get yourself registered as a local taxpayer. You will find further details of the documents you need in chapter 6.

Buying a property in the planning stage or under development

This will usually be at a lower price than a newly built house and you can sometimes have some of your own ideas incorporated in the construction. As with any kind of building work, you should always make sure you are purchasing from solid companies and only pay according to the development of the work, never in advance.

Buying a house under construction is a little more complicated. You should ask to see a copy of the Municipal Building Licence and the payment slip for it, and check out the guarantees for the completion of the infrastructure ie the roads, water supply and electricity supply.

If you buy a property that is at planning stage or under construction, it is very important that you get the guarantee that the law (Law 57 of 1968) entitles you to. This guarantee can be given in the form of a bank *aval* or an insurance policy, and will ensure that you get the money back if the property is not finished on the completion date that the promoter stipulates in the contract. You will find further details in chapter 8.

Buying a plot

If you are really adventurous you can buy a plot of land and build your house on it. Naturally, the legal niceties should be taken care of in connection with the house construction (see chapter 7) but, in addition, you will need to know a lot more about the land itself. Never assume that just because land is for sale that it can automatically be built on.

- All the land in Spain is subject to a law ruling what can be built on it, the activities for which it cannot be used etc.
- Every inch of land is intended for a certain type of use depending on its classification under the law.
- The law is a general rule and so there are detailed plans and rules issued by the local authorities relating to land in their area.

Plans and rules are public documents and can be consulted in the local Town Hall (the *Ayuntamiento*). The local Town Hall divides all the ground in each municipal area into three groups:

1 **Urban land** – land on which it is possible to build because it has been approved for building purposes and because it has the necessary services available. This type of land is known as *finca urbana*.
2 **Urbanisable land** – land destined to be eventually built upon.
3 **Non-urbanisable land** – usually rural land (*finca rustica*) which is assigned for some productive purpose such as agriculture, forestry, mining or water supply or land which is to be preserved because of its high ecological value.

This is the reason why all construction is prohibited in some areas while in others only buildings destined for agricultural purposes can be built.

If building is allowed, then a permit can be obtained through a special procedure in which the Town Hall will play a part. If the licence is granted, the buildings will have to fit in with their surroundings ie you might find it difficult to build a town house in a rural area.

If you wish to buy a plot, you should first ask your lawyer to undertake some early investigations with the local Town Hall. The information that you need (and it should be in writing) is the classification given to the land, whether or not you are allowed to build there and the use to which the land may be put. Your lawyer will write to the Town Hall giving them the precise address of the property and asking for an *informe urbanistica* on the land. This may take some time to get but it will tell you for what purpose the land has been classified and whether or not it is building land or agricultural land.

If you are buying a plot on an urbanisation, then it's important to get confirmation from the Town Hall that the urbanisation is legal and all the necessary infrastructure (ie roads) is going to be provided. You should also get confirmation that the property to be built is legal in itself and you will find that some Town Halls have strict rules on the dimensions of properties that can be built on various plots (not only in terms of area covered but also in terms of total volume). If the property you are buying is likely to be covered by the Laws of Horizontal Property (see chapter 14) then you should find out if a community of owners exists and, if so, obtain a copy of their statutes to see if these restrict your building plans in any way.

If the property is agricultural land, then you need more information from the Town Hall. Local planning rules may not allow any kind of dwellings to be constructed on the land and, if they do, they may have strict minimum requirements on the size of plot on which dwellings can be built. Once again, you will need to get information about how big the house can be (both in terms of area and volume) and you must also get confirmation either from the Town Hall or via the Town Hall that you will get all the services you need such as roads, water, electricity and so on.

If you're thinking of buying a plot near the coast, then you should be aware that in the summer of 1988, a new 'law of the coasts' was approved by the Spanish Parliament. This law was aimed at protecting what remains of the coastline from further development and, although some aspects of the law are under appeal, a good deal of building work that was too close to the beach has been stopped and many plots that were at one time scheduled for building cannot now be built upon. So, if you're looking at land that is close to the beach, make sure that you enquire very carefully whether or not it falls under the new laws.

Obtaining a building licence

Once you know you may build on your plot, you must then apply for a building licence also from the local Town Hall. It will be granted if what you intend to do is in agreement with the local planning rules – if it isn't, it will be refused. In all cases, therefore, it is probably worthwhile visiting the Town Hall yourself and trying to get hold of the official in charge of granting planning permits to make sure that they are in favour of granting permission for your particular house. And make sure that you get your answer in writing.

The application for a building licence is made on an official application form together with a copy of the outline plans drawn up by your architect (and officially stamped by the college of architects) together with the title deed (the *escritura*) for the land.

Once the building licence has been granted, it lapses after eight months if work hasn't started and it is valid only for the time period stated in the licence, after which it must be renewed. If you have to renew your licence because building hasn't started, then you will have to pay a renewal fee of 20% of the original cost of the licence.

The cost of a licence may vary from area to area. For a small house the cost will be in the region of 12,000 pesetas; for larger properties it may be over double that.

The final thing to take note of is that when the licence is granted, a poster has to be erected on the building site showing the date the licence was granted, the start and finishing date for the building, the name of the licence holder and the name of the architect and *aparejador* (see later under 'Dealing with the architect').

A new building tax

At the end of 1988, a new tax was introduced. It is charged on all types of construction work, whether a building licence has been obtained or not, and is charged at the rate of 2% of the cost (although in larger municipalities the rate could be as high as 4%).

The person liable to pay the tax is the owner of the land, or the builder or whoever applies for the licence. At the end of the day, of course, the new tax will be passed on to the buyer.

The different types of land

If you really are serious about buying a plot, then it's important to know a little bit more about the technicalities. First of all, you must know the difference between a *finca rustica* and *finca urbana*. A *finca urbana* is land earmarked for construction; a *finca rustica* is agricultural land.

Finca urbana

By and large, it's going to be less difficult to get permission to build upon land earmarked for construction. Nevertheless, it isn't necessarily straightforward due to changes in town planning, the intervention of other authorities, inadequate or failing infrastructure (ie roads) and so on. Once again, you must get a building licence from the Town Hall and include in the contract a clause that will give you all your money back if the house that you intend to build on the plot cannot be built.

If the urbanisation where you buy is already authorised, the plans for it will specify the height of construction which is permitted on your plot, the total volume of the house, the distance your house must be from the road and the distance it must be from the boundaries of your neighbours' plots. These limitations are matters for a skilled professional to handle and you should engage an architect to make a pre-study so that you can be completely sure that you can build the house you want on the plot before buying it. You can then include a proper drawing of your planned house in the purchasing contract and make the purchase conditional upon the acceptance of this plan by the authorities.

Finca rustica

With a *finca rustica*, (and this is for the **really** adventurous) you have to be even more careful when buying land. Legally, you can build only for agricultural purposes but in some areas, the local Town Halls are issuing building permits for dwellings on such land. However, you could well find that the house you want to build can only be built on a plot of a certain size. It's as well to check this out before you buy the plot – if the plot you buy is too small, it will be useless for building purposes and you may have difficulty selling it to someone else.

If you want to build on a *finca rustica*, you must also make sure that you will get water, electricity, road access and (eventually) the telephone if you want it. Don't trust verbal assurances, make sure to get it in writing. Only the questions you ask will be answered so take nothing for granted and work out your questions carefully.

It's not unusual to have to rely on your own well for water so have a test boring made to determine the amount and quality for the water. If you are intending to link up with a main water supply, be sure to find out whether this will be allowed and whether you will be granted permission to lay a pipe on other people's property that has to be crossed.

The electricity line near to, or crossing your land may or may not be at the right voltage and it may or may not be permitted to make a direct connection to it. It's essential to consult the local electricity company not only for permission but also to find out about the costs of any transformers, poles and transmission lines that may be needed.

To build access roads to more important roads, you need permission from the authorities. If you have to cross other people's property, you need their written consent. There may be a road nearby that you are planning to use for access. But check first – is it really a public road or is it a private one? When investigating the property register, make sure that no-one else has rights of way over your land.

Dealing with the architect

If you're going to build a property from scratch and you have a plot in mind, your first task will be to employ an architect and an *aparejador*. The *aparejador* has no precise British equivalent – he may be thought of as an architectural technician or a building surveyor. Some architectural practices work in close collaboration with an *aparejador*; other *aparejadores* are totally independent.

Don't contract with any architect until you've made sure that he's able to design the house that you want and that you're able to build the house that he can design. Ask him to make a draft plan (*anteproyecto*) of the house that you have in mind and then find out if there are any problems in having this property built on the plot you intend to buy. If there are no problems, you can then contract with the architect to draw up the complete architectural plans and building specifications which should then be made an integral part of the building contract (see chapter 6).

It's important for you to discuss the potential house plans with your architect in considerable detail. It's important for you because you might be living in the property for some time and it's important for him because he's going to send you a bill of around 10% of the building costs. For that type of expenditure, you are entitled to expect time and commitment from him both in preparation of the plans and also in controlling the building of the property.

The sort of things that you should discuss with him could contain some items which are not entirely familiar to you if you have been used to living in the UK:

Go to the plot and discuss the siting of the house with the architect. Spain can be quite hilly – and it's not at all unusual to have to build a house on sloping ground (in which case you should check the likely cost for extra foundations and retaining walls).

Work out what the views will be. Much of life in Spain is spent sitting on terraces in the sunshine – you need to know what you're going to be looking at.

You will need to be able to protect your house (and yourself) against the fierce heat of the sun in summer but you also want to get as much sun into the house as possible in the winter.

Don't forget that you probably intend to spend a fair bit of time outside your home, perhaps sitting on a terrace. Is there room for a terrace? Does it have adequate illumination? Is the terrace sheltered from the prevailing winds (which can blow with some force in the coastal areas)?

Think about how much space you and your family will need not only today but in the years to come. Your home may be built for holidays but even on holiday you need wardrobes and cupboard space. Even though you may not plan to spend much time in the kitchen, remember that you are probably going to want a breakfast and so a reasonable size kitchen area could be a blessing.

You will need to avoid steep and narrow stairs if you are infirm or getting on in years.

Find ways of diverting water away from the house when it rains (because when it rains in Spain, it can be very heavy indeed).

Try to make as much use as possible of traditional building styles and local materials.

Consider the possibility of using solar heating, collecting rainwater for watering the garden and the recycling of grey water (ie bath water).

Think about heating the house in winter and make sure that you have a fireplace that works.

Think about keeping the house cool in summer and work out the airflow through the house (ie getting a cool breeze flowing through the rooms).

Think about having an extra water tank installed.

Think carefully about the siting of light fittings, switches and electrical power points both inside and outside the house.

Take into consideration the height of working surfaces both in the kitchens and bathrooms. Spanish people tend, on average, to be slightly shorter than people from the UK and they tend in some cases to site their working surfaces slightly lower than usual.

Think about the security of your house and put iron grilles on all external doors and windows and consider installing a safe. Make sure your doors are strong.

And don't forget the greatest problem in most Spanish houses is the insulation against water, heat and cold. It's not unusual to find houses built into hillsides and also built on rock. The water flow down a rocky hillside can be quite substantial and the last thing you need is areas in the construction where water can be trapped. If you have a roof terrace (a *solarium*) make sure that it's well insulated against water penetration. All your terraces should slope well away from the house. Try and ensure that you have roof overhangs to protect windows and doors.

The summers can be hot – and sun coming through a large window can make the inside of a house like a furnace. Consider having blinds built into the window constructions and don't forget to think about mosquito netting. There's nothing worse on a hot summer's night than being unable to open the windows to let in some cool air because of the invasion by insects.

The winters can be damp and cold on the Spanish coastline. Having well insulated walls may seem like something you only need to think about in the UK – it's something to think about in Spain as well.

Once you've agreed with your architect what the plan should be, you then need to ask him to prepare a full description of building materials (*memoria de calidades*) and this together with the plan forms an integral part of the building contract (see chapter 6).

6 Dealing with the developer

The buying process

There are two ways in which you can buy a new property from a developer:

1 You can buy one ready built or one that is in course of construction.
2 You can buy a plot of land and have a dwelling built on it.

There are understandably a number of other areas that need to be taken into account in addition to the purely legal aspects in order to make sure that everything goes according to plan:

- You need to be clear about planning permission ie that the developer is permitted to build the house he wishes to sell you.
- You should consider buying the land in advance.
- You need a good contract with the developer.
- You need to be sure that, when the property is completed, you will get access to services you need (roads, water, electricity) and that the property (when it is finished) has been correctly constructed and is fit to live in.

Planning permission

You will find planning considerations covered in detail in the previous chapter – this is to remind you of the basic requirements. If you are buying a plot and arranging for a house to be built yourself, then you will be attending to these requirements personally. If, on the other hand, you are buying a house in the course of construction, then you will need to be reassured that your builder has attended to all the necessary requirements.

The main requirements are as follows:

- You must be absolutely clear about planning permission ie that the house as designed may be built on the plot that has been purchased and that there is nothing illegal about the development.
- The builder should be in possession of the complete building plans and schedule of building materials (*memoria de calidades*). These will have been drawn up by the architects and will have been signed by them and stamped by the College of Architects.
- Finally, you should make sure that you have sight of either the building licence issued by the Town Hall or an authorised photocopy of the licence. This is the document which gives the builder permission to build the house which the architect has designed.

Buying the land

Unless you are buying a completed new house (ie one that is ready to move into) then you will be waiting for some time either for the house to be built or for the house to be finished. In these cases, it is a very good idea to buy the land first so that at least you have the protection that if anything goes seriously wrong, the land is yours. You may find that the builder (if he is the owner of the land) may also ask you to sign an exclusive contract for the construction of the property as well. This clearly restricts your freedom of action but it's not entirely unreasonable. However, it's likely that the builder will ask you to sign the building contract before going through the formalities of making the *escritura* for the land so it's most important that the contract does not in any way inhibit you from obtaining the *escritura*.

For example, some builders will often propose in their contracts that you will only get title to the property when all the money has been paid over (ie both for the plot and for the construction). This is really quite dangerous because you would not have any legal protection at all for the money that you've paid out if the builder goes into liquidation while the house is being built (and that is not at all unknown). What you should ensure is that the building contract contains a clause which stipulates that no building work will take place and no payments for any building work will be made until you get title to the land.

The other reason for having a separate contract is purely financial. If the plot belongs to the builder, then this may be used as a lever to request additional payment for the construction (ie over and above the agreed price) and you may have difficulty getting all the necessary documents when construction is complete unless you make these extra payments. If you own the plot, then the builder has no lever for demanding extra payment (although he does, of course, have the full backing of the law in getting you to pay the agreed price for the construction).

The final reason for buying the land first is that there may be tax advantages (see chapter 10).

The building contract

Reservations and options

On your very first meeting with the developer (and this may even happen when you have your first meeting with the sales agent) you may be asked to sign a piece of paper 'to reserve the house for you'. This is generally to put you under some kind of obligation and there is usually no need to sign anything. However, in some cases, you may prefer to go back to the UK knowing that you have some kind of hold over the property that took your fancy. However, do be sure that you know exactly what you are signing:

- A **reservation** is simply to reserve a plot or property for, say, two weeks while you make up your mind. There should be no need to pay over any money but if you do, make sure that it is returnable in full if you decide not to go ahead. There is no law in Spain to cover the concept of reservations so you have no legal redress if things go wrong. At the same time, make sure the reservation you sign is just that and not a contract to purchase in disguise (it has been known!). Don't sign anything that is only in Spanish – insist on a translation.
- An **option** to buy a property **is** covered by law and if you pay over any money you may have difficulty recovering it if you withdraw from the deal. At the same time, you should note that the option is legally binding as far as the specific dwelling is concerned; make sure, therefore, that you understand the details of the final purchase contract before you sign the option.

The form of the contract

A contract of sale/purchase between two able parties (where the property sold/bought is mentioned together with the price) is legal and binding on both parties. Even a verbal agreement that can be proved is binding. If you pay a sum of money, and a receipt is given saying 'received from Mr X the sum of 300,000 pesetas as first payment for the purchase of house' it is a contract. When a legal and binding contract is not complied with by one of the two contracting parties, the other can either demand fulfilment through the courts, or agree to the cancellation on certain terms (the vendor keeping all or part of the payments made by the purchaser so far).

There is one type of contract however that can legally be cancelled. That is if the first payment is made in the form of *arras*. The Spanish word *arras* can be translated as **deposit**. Sometimes the word *señal* is used in the same concept, translated as **token**. In such cases the article 1454 of the Spanish Civil Code applies where it states: 'If a deposit or token payment has been agreed in the purchasing contract, the contract can be dissolved by the purchaser renouncing the deposit, or the vendor by paying back double the amount'.

If you are a buyer, and the vendor proposes a contract containing the terms *arras, señal, deposit, token payment* or similar expressions, you know that he wishes to reserve for himself the right to back out of the contract if he finds a buyer who wishes to pay a higher price, or if he cannot deliver, (maybe because he has no title to the property himself). Of course, this kind of contract will also give you the right to withdraw from the arrangements if you do not wish to proceed but you should bear in mind that under these circumstances you will lose your deposit.

Preliminary work

On the assumption that you have purchased a plot on your own initiative or from a local agent or developer you are now ready to build your house on it.

We will also assume that you've obtained the necessary planning permission, that the architect has drawn up plans and a schedule of building materials and that the necessary building licence has been issued by the Town Hall.

You are now in a position to start choosing a builder. When you start choosing a builder, take your time. Ask for prices from more than one reputable builder (your architect will help you here) and look at houses they have built before making your choice (and talk with the owners if possible). Check that you are actually contracting with the builder himself and not with the middle man (occasionally, some people make building contracts with clients as if they were the real builders and then sub-contract the building to another builder).

The contract itself

Never sign a contract if you don't fully understand it and don't pay out any money on it until you do. Ask for a correct and signed version in English and if the builder can't do that for you, get it translated yourself. The sort of details that the contract should cover are as follows:

- It should contain the name and address of the builder. If it is a company, then the place and the date of registration should be given as well together with the authority of the person signing the contract.
- It should clearly identify the property.
- It should state that the construction will be on the basis of the plans of the architect (and you should ensure that the plans and the schedule of building quantities and qualities are signed by the architect and included as part of the contract).
- It should specify the size of the house (in square metres). Make sure the figure relates to living space. Occasionally you may find that it includes the terrace, solarium etc, which is misleading.

- It must specify the total price and also what is and what is not included in the total price such as:
  — Service connections
  — Retaining walls
  — Entrance drive
  — Landscaping
  — Swimming pool with machinery
  — Fireplace
  — Exterior stairs and rails
  — Window grilles
  — Lamps
  — Kitchen equipment
  — Bathroom equipment
  — Solar heating installation
  — Additional water storage tank
- It should contain an agreed date by which the building should be finished and should also (if relevant) indicate a date by which the work will be started. There should also be a clause incorporating a penalty for the builder to pay if the property is not finished in time.
- It would be normal to pay a certain percentage of the total building price in advance so that the builder can buy materials (but this should not be more than, say, 30% of the total).
- It should contain a schedule of payments according to the phase of construction and not fixed dates. The money stipulated for each phase should be paid against certificates supplied by the architect.
- The builder will insist on a clause which will charge you interest if the payments are late.
- There should be a clause indicating that at the same time as the final payment, the keys will be handed over together with the certificate of electrical installation, the certificate of finished work from the architect and the certificate of habitability.
- The contract should specify whether or not the price includes *IVA*, the cost of the building licence and the fees of the architect and *aparejador*.

There should also be a clause enabling you to retain up to

10% of the total building costs for up to six months after completion as security for the repair of any defects you find. The law in Spain gives you additional protection in that the builder is responsible for hidden defects in the construction for a period of ten years.

The architect is responsible for the same period of time if the defects result from the ground on which your home is built (eg subsidence) or if the defects are due to the instructions given to the builder relating to the construction of the house. The time period of ten years is extended to 15 years if the builder has constructed the house in a way which is in breach of contract.

The basic recommendation is that you should not accept a period of less than six months for the correction of faults and you should get your own architect or *aparejador* to report on the faults and to suggest the ways in which they might be corrected. Once faults are detected, you certainly shouldn't delay in letting the builder know. You should, of course, let him know in writing and if you get no reply, you can engage the help of a notary and send the builder a letter as a *requirimiento notarial*. Your builder will then be obliged to act.

In the same way, you can ask for a notary to view the defects in your home and ask him to attest them in an *acta notarial*.

The documents on completion

When the house is completed, there are three key documents that you will need to get from the builder:

- The first of these is the *certificado de fin de obra*. This literally means the certificate of finished work and it is issued by the architect and the *aparejador* and stamped by their respective colleges. This is official confirmation from them that the house has been built in the way that the plans stipulated.

- You must also obtain the *cedula de habitabilidad*. That literally means the certificate of habitability and it's issued by the Town Hall or higher authorities declaring that the house is fit for living in.
- The third document you need is the *boletin de instalaciones electricas*. This is a certificate of electrical installation issued by the electrician who has done the wiring of the house and without this, you will not be able to get the electricity company to connect the electrical supply to the house.

It is for this reason that the handing over of these documents should be part of the contract. Without these documents you will be unable to take up occupation of your house and some builders could well use this as an excuse for requesting payment for 'extras'. If the contract contains the agreed price plus the fact that the documents will be handed over when the price has been paid, the builder will have no option other than to hand over the documents so that you may take possession of your property.

When the house is finally finished you can then arrange to make the final payment to the builder and at the same time go to the notary and get the *declaracion de obra nueva* prepared which is the *escritura* for the house on the plot that you have bought.

You now have everything you need to take up occupation of your house and the next stage is to take all the documents that you've been issued with to the Town Hall and register yourself as a local taxpayer so that you can start paying local rates.

7 Understanding the legalities

Introduction

One of the most fundamental aspects of buying property in Spain is that the ownership of **land** is all important. Whoever owns the land owns what is built on it. Consequently, ownership of land is very important in the Spanish system and land is often used as security to cover mortgages and other debts. Until the debt is repaid, it becomes a completely integral part of all subsequent transactions involving the land and means that if you buy land that has a mortgage registered against it, then you become responsible for repaying the mortgage.

In all property transactions in Spain, therefore, it is most important to ensure that not only do you have good title to the land (ie that you own the land and therefore everything that's put on it) but also that there are no mortgages or debts outstanding on the property that you might inherit when you buy the land.

All this information is contained in the property register which is an integral part of the legal system involving the purchase of property. Making sure that you do have good title to the property is no work for the amateur and it is **strongly** recommended that you engage legal help to do this. The equivalent to a UK solicitor in Spain is known as an *abogado* and you will normally be able to find English speaking *abogados* in most of the main tourist centres in Spain. Alternatively, you can go to your solicitor in the UK and ask him to check in the register of solicitors for the names of *abogados* practising in the UK. There are a few and they are usually attached to a London firm of solicitors.

When buying property in the UK, you can expect your solicitor to undertake all of the necessary legal work involved in the conveyancing and you may well have means of redress if he fails to do the job properly. No such means exist **in the UK** for taking action against a Spanish lawyer. If any problems subsequently arise you may find it difficult to obtain redress or to get the problem sorted out.

To some extent therefore, there are some advantages in using a London based *abogado* attached to a UK firm of solicitors because they at least will operate in a way which is more in keeping with UK standards. Nevertheless, it still pays to make quite sure that you and he understand exactly what you expect him to do. The *abogado* will of course advise you on what should be done – and you should listen carefully to what he has to suggest.

The basic legal system

The most common word you will hear in dealing with property purchases in Spain is the *escritura*. This means 'deed' and there are all kinds of *escrituras* in the Spanish legal system. The one in connection with property purchase is called the *escritura de compraventa* which roughly translates as the title deeds or the conveyance. At the end of the day, it is this document which will prove your title to the property in the event of any dispute.

The very first stage therefore in any property transaction in Spain is a simple check to make sure that the person selling you the property is the owner of the land and that there are no outstanding debts on it. The person selling you the land should supply you with a copy of his *escritura* which will show the official address of the property and the registration number of the property in the property register. If you give these details to your *abogado*, he will write to the local property register and ask for a *nota simple*. The property registry will then provide details of the size of the property, the name of the actual owner and whether or not there are any incumbrances (ie outstanding mortgages or debts) on it.

This first simple check should be carried out as early as possible in the transaction in order that you can avoid major problems later on.

If you are buying a second-hand house or a new house that has already been built, then the *escritura de compraventa* may cover both the land and all the buildings that have been constructed on that land. If, however, you are buying a plot of land on which you intend to build or are buying a plot of land on which there is a house partially constructed, then it would be usual to carry out the transaction in two stages:

1   The first stage is to get the *escritura* of the land as soon as possible. You can, of course, only do this by paying for the land in full but this is your guarantee that you at least will own the property which is built on the land.
2   When the building work is completed, you obtain a *declaracion de obra nueva* (which literally means declaration of new work). This takes the form of a further *escritura* which describes the property which has been built on the particular plot of land.

The legal process

In England, the signing of the various documents by the buyer and seller can take place at different places and at different times, often with each party doing it in the presence of their own legal adviser. In Spain, the signing is done in front of a notary, a public official whose job it is to record an agreement that has already been reached between the buyer and seller. The notary will draw up the *escritura* and then it is signed in front of him by you and the seller.

As a purchaser, you can either sign the *escritura* yourself or you can give someone else (a lawyer, a member of your family or a trusted friend), a power of attorney (a *poder general*) to sign on your behalf. Occasionally you may be asked by the promoter or sales organisation to give them or someone in their office a power of attorney to sign the *escritura* on your behalf. You must use your own judgment on this but it's not recommended because a power of attorney may be phrased in general terms. This, in an extreme case, could permit them to change the purchasing contract as well which is probably something you wouldn't wish them to do.

One alternative is to allow the company to name someone as a verbal representative to represent you when the *escritura* is signed. You must then ratify the *escritura* yourself later on but this can be done at a Spanish consulate in the UK and doesn't necessarily have to be done in Spain. In that way, you retain the right to control events without holding up the signing of the *escritura* by the promoter.

If you are paying for your property via a mortgage (specifically through a Spanish bank), then you will generally make the first payment to the promoter, with the balance being paid by the bank on your behalf. The bank will allow the *escritura* to be made in your name but it will, of course, contain a mortgage in the bank's favour. This is normally sufficient security for the bank but they may also request that they hold onto the top copy of the *escritura* for safe keeping. When you pay the final instalment on your mortgage to the bank, they will cancel the mortgage and, if necessary, arrange for the *escritura* to be returned to you. If you are paying for your property out of your own resources, but in stages (for example if you are buying a property which is still under construction), it is important to get the *escritura* at the same time as you make the final payment.

In some cases, you may be told that it is not possible to get the *escritura* handed over at the same time as the final payment is made on the grounds that getting the necessary bank certificate may take a few days. The solution is to get, from your bank, a cheque in convertible *pesetas* and to ask the bank to write on the back of the cheque a note of confirmation that this payment is for the purchase of a specified property. A photocopy of this cheque will be included by the notary, as the equivalent of a bank certificate in the escritura which can then be signed. You will find full details of the financial aspects in chapter 8.

Selling your property in the UK

If you sell your property to somebody else in the UK, then it may be possible to arrange to have the *escritura* signed at a Spanish consulate in the UK if this is more convenient. The consul acts as a notary but he will require all the usual identification papers (principally passports) and the previous *escritura* of the property. You will then have to get the *escritura* to the property register for registration and you must get it there within 30 days. If you want to take the *escritura* to the property register for registration yourself, you must always get what is called the '*primera copia*' (literally the top copy), which is signed by the two parties and witnessed by the notary. A photocopy, what is called a '*copia simple*', cannot be registered.

The role of the notary

The role of the notary is to confirm officially that all the legal niceties have been attended to in connection with the sale of the property. It is normal to send all the papers to the notary who will then prepare the *escritura*. When it is ready for signing, the notary will read it to you (and if you don't understand Spanish he is obliged to have an interpreter present) and he will then invite you to sign. When you have signed it, the notary will sign it and he will then give you a copy of what you have signed, called the *copia simple*.

However, you **must** be aware of what you have signed.

The notary, is a public official who is merely **witnessing** an agreement. He does not know, and it is not his job to know, whether the information in the *escritura* is correct or even complete. What he signs is '*yo doy fe*' which literally means 'I give in faith' ie 'I certify'.

The sorts of thing that can still go wrong at this stage are, for example:

- The seller, having cashed your cheque, can take another buyer to another notary's office and make another *escritura*. If the second *escritura* gets to the property registry first then that is the one which will be inscribed in the register.
- The seller might take out a mortgage on the property after he has sold it to you, or his creditors (the tax collector for example) might put an embargo on the property after the *escritura* has been issued.

In such cases, the property registrar might refuse to enter the *escritura* (if another buyer was faster than you in getting his *escritura* to the register) or he may register it, but adding that the *escritura* has no effect on the embargo or mortgage already entered. Alternatively, he may register it and tell you nothing about the charges existing on the property. This is not a feature of life which is peculiar to foreigners buying property in Spain. It's a feature of the Spanish system of selling property and many Spaniards get caught as well.

There are four basic precautions that you can take:

1 Employ a reputable lawyer and choose one that is independent – not necessarily the lawyer suggested to you by the seller.
2 Instruct your lawyer to get an extract from the property register (the *nota simple*) **just before** you sign the *escritura*.
3 If you do not trust the vendor, do everything you can to make sure that the *escritura* gets to the property registry as soon as possible after you have signed it. You can do this by asking the notary to give you the *primera copia* so that you can take it yourself. When the property registry

receive it, they will mark on it the day and time of receipt. This is called an *asiento de presentacion* and it ensures that no other entries (such as a recent mortgage) can be inscribed in the register for 60 days (and this period can be lengthened if necessary for a further 180 days).

4   Ask your lawyer to keep in touch with the property registry to make sure that the *escritura* is definitely inscribed in the property register. Some registries are very busy and it can take a considerable amount of time.

Once the *escritura* is inscribed in the property register, the *primera copia* will be returned via the notary's office with a receipt for the taxes (*IVA* or *ITP* – see chapter 10) and the fees you have paid (which will be paid to the notary for his work and also to the property registry for their work). It will bear the property registry's official stamp which will show the book and the page where the inscription has been made.

You can now relax – the property is safely yours.

8 Paying for your property

Buying property involves money so it is important to make arrangements with a bank as soon as you are serious about buying your property – and to understand how the system works.

The basic rules

When you buy property in Spain, the general rule is that it must be paid for in foreign currency. This establishes your right to take your currency out of Spain again if you should sell your property. The original amount will be adjusted according to a formula laid down by the Ministry of Commerce to compensate you for inflation but any excess over that will have to be retained in Spain.

It will be necessary for you to prove that you imported foreign currency which has then been exchanged into *pesetas* and you do this by means of a bank certificate. This will then be attached to the title deed (or mentioned in it) and that is sufficient proof that you have abided by the rules.

You are allowed to buy property from a non-resident and pay him outside Spain in any currency he will accept. Provided there is a bank certificate mentioned in the deed relating to the previous purchase, you will then acquire the foreign currency rights of the previous owner. However, you won't acquire the foreign currency rights in respect of the excess if he sells you the property at a higher price than the value shown in his bank certificate.

However, with the European Community becoming a real Common Market, the Spanish foreign currency restrictions will eventually be lifted and the problems of the bank certificate will be solved.

The purchase of property

The simplest way to buy your property in Spain is to use a convertible *peseta* account and to request the bank to give you a bank certificate. This is particularly important if you are a non-resident. If you are buying from a Spanish individual or company, or from a foreigner who doesn't have a bank certificate mentioned in the *escritura*, you **must** get a bank certificate yourself because without it, the notary is not allowed to prepare the title deeds for you.

To get the certificate, you need to be able to show that your importation of currency was sufficiently recent for it to be required for a specific purpose and you must also be able to specify the details of the property that you intend to purchase. Your bank will not be allowed to give you a certificate in request of currency imported a long time ago or if you are unable to give them the address of the property you intend to purchase.

Obtaining a bank certificate

The normal procedure for obtaining a bank certificate is to open an account in convertible *pesetas* at the bank of your choice and then get the funds sent from your own UK bank to cover your needs. If you give your UK bank full details of your convertible account, there should be no problems and the money should normally be available within a few working days.

You must then approach your Spanish bank and tell them that you wish them to issue a convertible *peseta* cheque to buy property. They will need the name of the seller (note, not the agent) together with his identity number (if he is Spanish) or his passport details (if he's not Spanish). The bank will also need the seller's address.

The bank will then prepare the bank certificate. They will need your name and proof of identity, the total sum in *pesetas* that you are paying, and the details of the property you are buying (and if you are buying second-hand property, the simplest way is to let them have a copy of the previous *escritura*). You then have a cheque and the bank certificate and so you are now ready to go to the notary to make the *escritura*. The certificate will be needed at an early stage (in order that the deeds may be prepared) but you won't be expected to actually hand over the cheque until you sign the deeds.

Usually, the sales company will send details of the transaction to the Director General of Foreign Transactions in Madrid. Provided the Ministry are happy about the transaction (and that is usually just a formality) they will confirm it with form TE7. The notaries will require sight of form TE7 before they complete the formation of the title deeds (see chapter 7).

Paying for your property in stages

If you are buying new property in the course of construction, then there is nothing unusual in paying for your property in stages. This is a common custom in Spain just as it is in the UK. All that you need to do here is to ensure that your bank makes a note of each stage payment in the same way, and then ask them to supply a bank certificate when the time comes to make the final payment. Your bank, of course, will not make any investigation to make sure the payment is due. It is up to you to make sure that the builder is keeping to the terms of his agreement, although this could be done by asking the architect to approve the payments as they become due.

Buying an apartment

There is a particular degree of protection given you if you are buying from a developer who is selling 'multi-unit dwellings' eg a block of flats. If the developer asks for any payment before the property is completed, he must give you a bank guarantee for all payments that you make to him. This guarantee ensures that all the money you pay over, plus 6% interest, will be paid back to you if your apartment is not completed within the agreed time limit. This guarantee is called an *aval bancario* and is covered by an insurance policy or by a bank. The developer is obliged to keep all the money paid by you in a special account and musn't use it for any purpose other than building the property.

This is particularly important to you if you are buying an apartment in an unfinished block. You should make sure that the legal requirements are contained in the purchasing contract which should also contain a clause stating that all the money you pay will be returned plus interest. This money should be returned to you not only if the property isn't finished within a certain time limit but also if the builder doesn't supply you with the necessary certificate of habitability.

The law is very much on your side in this kind of situation. If the developer has not taken out the insurance policy (ie the *aval bancario*), then he is breaking the law.

One of the leading companies in this area is Credito y Caucion, who specialise in this form of insurance. Their office is in Madrid (Raimundo Fernandez Villaverde, 61 – Apartado de Correos 524).

Paying by *letras*

Another method of stage payment is to pay by what are called *letras*. What this means is that you sign post-dated promissory notes for each instalment and instruct your bank to pay them as they become due. There are of course problems – if the builder has not completed the work that he is due to complete by a certain date, you have paid him and there is no going back on the deal. If you attempt to prevent payment then you could be in trouble because non-payment of a *letra* is a serious offence in Spain and your assets can be embargoed or confiscated to enforce payment.

The safe route is not to sign *letras* if at all possible. It's far better to agree with the builder a schedule of payments upon completion of various stages and then to make payment at each stage. Although your bank can't take responsibility for the fact that building is at the correct stage, it should be possible to persuade the architect or other responsible official to provide the bank with a certificate of satisfactory progress which is some protection that the work has been done before you pay for it. The only alternative, of course, is to go and see for yourself.

Borrowing money to pay for your property

If you are unable to finance the purchase of your property out of your own cash resources, you will have to borrow the money. There are basically three options open to you:

1   You can raise a mortgage in the UK using your UK assets
     as security.
2   You can raise a mortgage in the UK using your Spanish
     property as security.
3   You can raise a mortgage in Spain using your Spanish
     property as security.

UK loans against UK assets

With the rapid increase in house prices this decade, people
who have owned a home here for more than a year or two
may well have a considerable amount of equity in their
property. This equity can be released by means of a re-
mortgage or through a further advance and the proceeds used
for the purchase of a second home abroad. In general, a
mortgage on UK property will offer a wider choice of options
than a mortgage using the foreign property as security.

The key advantages of raising a loan against UK property are
as follows:

● It allows you to pay for your Spanish property in cash
   which could make things very much simpler should you
   at any time in the future decide to sell your Spanish
   property and repatriate the proceeds.
● UK mortgages are commonly granted for longer terms
   than may generally be obtained from foreign banks. For
   non-residents, a maximum term of 15 years is common
   in many European countries – in the UK, terms of 25
   years are commonplace and even terms in excess of 30
   years are possible.
● The loan is granted and repayable in sterling so there is
   no exchange rate risk (which could arise if the loan was
   granted and payable in foreign currency).
● There are no withholding tax problems for UK residents
   (see later section).
● UK interest rates are often lower than those obtainable
   from banks in the most popular areas for homes abroad
   including Spain.

- UK lending institutions offer a rather more flexible approach to repayment methods than many European banks who will often consider only a straight repayment mortgage.

If you decide to use your existing UK home as the security for a further loan, then you will have to decide whether or not to re-mortgage your property or apply for a further advance. Your first call should be to your current lender (if you are buying your UK home on a mortgage) but it may be necessary to apply to another lender if you need a further advance. In most cases, lenders obviously require adequate security and will normally prefer a first charge on your UK property. However, an increasing number of lenders are prepared to accept a second charge behind another lender although this will usually mean a higher rate of interest.

One important thing to bear in mind when applying for a re-mortgage is the question of tax relief. The rules for mortgage tax relief were modified in the 1988 Finance Act to exclude relief for home improvement loans. If you have an existing loan with a home improvement element on it on which you are obtaining tax relief, the relief on the home improvement element will be lost if the loan is varied, for example by a re-mortgage. Consequently, before deciding to re-mortgage your UK property in order to raise capital to buy a property abroad, you should make quite sure that the tax relief on your existing loan will not be affected in any way.

Even if your existing tax relief is unaffected by the change, adding a non-qualifying loan (and a loan to buy property abroad **is** a non-qualifying loan ie it does not qualify for tax relief on the interest) to your existing mortgage will take the whole loan out of the MIRAS system. This is a factor to be borne in mind if you are self-employed because you will only be able to claim the tax relief on the qualifying part of your mortgage through your tax return.

Another change in the 1988 Finance Act was the restriction of mortgage relief to £30,000 per property, thus ruling out 'double MIRAS' for unmarried couples. The restriction applies to loans effected after 1 August 1988 but existing arrangements are unaffected. It is likely to make good sense, therefore, not to disturb an arrangement that attracts this valuable benefit.

A further advance means asking your existing lender for more funds and while most lenders will be willing to consider this, they may charge you an increased rate of interest for the further advance. In favour of a further advance, there is the fact that you have a pre-existing relationship with your current lender and this should stand you in good stead when applying for the extra money. A re-mortgage could well mean transferring your mortgage to a new lender which will inevitably mean extra costs for legal and valuation fees.

It may, of course, be perfectly acceptable to raise a UK loan against other security and many banks will consider taking a wide range of investment holdings as loan security (eg shares, unit trusts, insurance bonds and so on). The principal disadvantage of this type of loan is that it's likely to be more difficult to arrange than a loan secured against property and its availability will be more dependent on the current financial climate. Also, the maximum loan is unlikely to exceed 60% of the value of the collateral (although it may be more for Government bonds and cash deposits). Also, you may well find that the loan is limited to a period of five years.

UK loans against Spanish assets

It is, of course, perfectly possible to use your foreign property as security for the loan. In theory, there is no reason why a lender in one country should not take as security a property situated in another country. In practice, however, this is unlikely to happen as lenders are often unwilling to take a charge under an unfamiliar legal system where (if the worst happens) obtaining permission to foreclose on the mortgage will have to be pursued in foreign courts.

However, you may find that your bank will accept a guarantee from a foreign bank and that the guarantee can be secured on the overseas property (but be prepared for a fee of about 1% a year for this guarantee).

Spanish loan against your Spanish property

The final method is to negotiate a loan with a lender based in Spain, using your Spanish home as security for the loan. If the bank in question has a branch in the UK which is prepared to grant the loan then some of the disadvantages can be avoided although you will still find yourself dealing with an unfamiliar lending system.

The principal disadvantages of this method are:

- The maximum loan available will often be no more than 60% of valuation (although some lenders will consider a loan of up to 75%).
- The term of the loan is likely to be considerably less than that available from a UK lender.
- The rates of interest are often higher than in the UK.
- The loan may be repayable in *pesetas* which introduces an exchange rate risk.
- The exchange control regulations in Spain mean that only currency which was correctly **imported** can later be repatriated. If you take a Spanish loan, it will not fall into the category of imported currency with the result that it may be difficult to repatriate the balance of the sale proceeds.
- There may be a liability to withhoiding tax.
- The nature of the security taken by a Spanish bank is often such that in the event of a default, the whole of the property reverts to the bank, not just the amount of your indebtedness.
- You may not be able to take advantage of the wide variety of repayment options acceptable to UK based lenders.
- Stage payments for new properties may not be obtainable.

The tax position

There are three main areas where it is important to understand the tax implications before proceeding with the purchase of your property.

Tax relief on the mortgage

Mortgage interest relief is granted against the interest paid on the first £30,000 of a 'qualifying loan' – either by deduction at source (the MIRAS system) or by adjustment to your personal tax code (and, for higher rate taxpayers, a combination of both methods).

A 'qualifying loan' is, for our purposes, a loan granted for the purchase of property in the United Kingdom which is your only or main residence.

Raising a loan to buy property abroad falls outside this definition and therefore UK tax relief is **not** available on the loan interest.

Tax relief against letting income

If you intend to let your property, the income that you receive will be liable to taxation both in the UK and also in Spain (although there may be relief available under the appropriate double taxation treaty). In the UK, if you own property which is available for letting as holiday accommodation, you are allowed to offset the interest that you pay on the loan against the income that you receive from letting. This only applies to UK property – it does **not** apply to foreign property.

Withholding tax

If you enter into any kind of loan agreement with a Spanish or other overseas bank, make absolutely certain that the loan agreement states that the interest rate that you pay is **after deduction of UK withholding taxes**. The reason for this is that if you pay annual interest to any individual or organisation, it is income in their hands and the Inland Revenue may require you to deduct tax at the basic rate from the interest payments. This ensures that the Inland Revenue get their share of the income that you are paying to the person from whom you have borrowed the money. The Revenue may want more money from the lender but they will sort that out themselves.

This principle still applies even if you pay interest abroad. In these circumstances, the tax that you have to deduct and pay to the Revenue is called 'withholding tax', (although under a double taxation agreement the amount of tax that you are required to deduct from the interest payments will normally be less than the standard rate of withholding tax). Nevertheless, if you have not made sure that your loan agreement states that the interest rate is after deduction of withholding taxes, you could find yourself paying the gross interest to the Spanish Bank and the withholding tax to the Inland Revenue.

The moral of this is – if you are looking for a loan from a Spanish Bank, make sure that you show the agreement to an accountant or solicitor who is familiar with withholding taxes to make sure that you end up paying only the agreed rate of interest and no more.

And don't rely on official ignorance to get you off the hook. The Spanish Inland Revenue are now giving the UK Inland Revenue details of UK residents who have borrowed in Spain and the Inland Revenue now have a special section in the tax return to record interest paid to a foreign bank.

Repayment methods

There are three principal methods of repaying a mortgage in the UK:

- The 'repayment' method where you make regular payments covering both interest and repayment of capital over the term of the mortgage.
- The 'endowment' method where you pay interest only throughout the term of the mortgage and repay the loan out of the proceeds of a suitable endowment life assurance policy.
- The 'pension related' method where you pay interest only throughout the term of the mortgage and repay the loan when you retire out of the lump sum that you may be eligible for under the terms of your pension plan.

Each of these methods has its advantages and disadvantages and you should discuss the method that is most appropriate to you with your usual financial adviser.

If you are borrowing money in the UK on the security of your UK property, you may well have considerable choice of mortgage repayment method. Borrowing against other security or borrowing from an overseas bank could mean that you are obliged to use the repayment terms dictated by the lender.

9 You and your bank account

Opening a bank account

In order to buy property in Spain, you need a bank account in Spain and the quickest way is to open a **convertible** *peseta* **account** with a bank near to the place that you are going to live. You will find that there are a number of Spanish banks with branches in London and in other major cities or, alternatively, you can go to your own UK bank, many of which have established branches in various parts of Spain. This is very straightforward and you are required only to provide a minimum amount of information about yourself. The bank will need to know the name of your mother and the name of your father and they'll also want details of your passport.

There is no problem with transferring sterling from the UK to Spain either from your existing UK bank or via a Spanish bank with a branch in London. You will have to pay the costs of conversion and you can also expect to pay a handling charge if sending cash by telex.

Operating a bank account in Spain is just like operating one in the UK. They are there to look after your cash needs and there are the usual provisions for depositing and withdrawing cash. You will be able to get a chequebook for your account and some banks also have cash cards to make it easier to get cash when you need it. You will also be able to set up standing orders in order to pay the regular electricity and water bills etc, that you are going to be required to pay once you settle down in your home.

There is one main difference between banking in this country and banking in Spain – and it's as well to get used to this as quickly as possible. Along with the telephone system, the banking system is the thing that most people love to hate about Spain. You just have to take it for granted that banking in Spain is going to be an essentially frustrating occupation. It is very bureaucratic and getting confirmation of even the most straightforward transactions can often take a considerable amount of time. Be prepared to be patient!

Banking rules

Banking for tourists

There are three types of bank account that a tourist can open:

— A foreigner's account in ordinary *pesetas*
— A foreigner's account in convertible *pesetas*
— Sterling and other foreign currency accounts.

Ordinary peseta account

An ordinary *peseta* account is just like a current account in the UK. It is an account that you will use for day-to-day expenses and it is this account on which you will draw cheques, arrange standing orders and have a cash card.

Convertible peseta accounts

These are similar to ordinary *peseta* accounts but they are clearly designated as having received foreign currency from abroad. Consequently, when you purchase your property using *pesetas* from a convertible account, you will at the same time get a bank certificate which clearly states that your foreign currency has been converted into *pesetas* which have then been paid into a Spanish bank account. This certificate is then used to prove to the notary that the cash has been correctly paid into Spain. It is therefore a simpler process than applying for permission to use the money from an ordinary account.

Sterling and other foreign currency accounts

These are very straightforward and can be opened by any tourist. You can have cheques paid into it direct from your bank in the UK or from any other bank accounts you hold in any other part of Europe. You can also buy foreign currency from your bank in the UK and transfer it to your foreign currency accounts in Spain.

Banking for residents

Once you have taken up residence (see chapter 8) you will no longer be able to hold the tourist accounts that you may have opened earlier. You will therefore have to close these and open a normal domestic *peseta* current account. You can credit this account with payments received from abroad (eg pensions or interest payments) but it is not freely convertible back into sterling. However, residents are permitted to buy foreign currency for specific purposes each year (travelling abroad would be an obvious example as would payments to dependants living in the UK). There's an annual limit to this but it is adequate for most purposes.

The movement of currency

Since Spain joined the European Community, the rules on movement of currency have been considerably eased. If you are a resident, it's now possible for you to buy up to 350,000 *pesetas* worth of foreign currency per person for a visit abroad and to do this for as many times a year as you like (although when you return to Spain, you should sell back to your bank any foreign currency over 50,000 *pesetas* worth brought back into the country). In addition, you can also take out up to 100,000 *pesetas* every time you leave Spain.

Tourists may purchase up to 100,000 *pesetas* worth of foreign currency when they leave Spain but for amounts over this, you must be able to prove that you've brought the money into Spain in the first place. You can also have up to 100,000 *pesetas* on you when leaving Spain.

Rules on cheques

New laws came into effect on 1 January 1986 regarding cheques. The most important points for foreigners are the following:

1 Post-dated cheques will be paid on presentation.
2 If you sign a cheque but don't have sufficient funds in your bank account, your bank is obliged to pay out whatever you have in your account as part payment towards the cheque.
3 Cheques are valid for six months from the date they are presented.
4 If you lose your chequebook through carelessness, you might find that the banks will not accept liability for any payments made through the fraudulent use of your chequebook. If, on the other hand, your chequebook has been stolen then you should notify the bank straightaway and they will accept liability for any subsequent clearances.

Bank accounts are still not totally accepted in Spain and a number of people still prefer cash. Consequently, if you are paying people in Spain, they will often ask you to make out a cheque *al portador* (ie to the bearer). This is just as good as cash in their hands – and you may be given one as well under some circumstances, so be careful not to lose it.

Standing orders

It's possible to pay a number of bills by standing order and it's recommended that you do. As an example, it is preferable to charge all local taxes and levies, electricity, oil, telephone, water and so on to your Spanish bank account.

Tell the offices that will be sending you the bills that you want to make a *domiciliacion bancaria*. Once you have signed the form, your bills will then be sent straight to your Spanish bank and they will pay them. They will then send the bill on to you but remember, it will not have been checked – you have to do this yourself.

It's also possible for a foreigner to have a cashcard on his Spanish bank account and you might find this a useful way of getting cash when you need it without having to queue. Also, if you are a resident, you can request a credit card on your Spanish bank account but you are well advised to keep all your statements relating to your credit card for at least three years. The Spanish authorities may occasionally require evidence that you haven't used it for excessive expenditure abroad (over and above your limits) so it's sensible to keep the proof.

10 The tax system – Part 1

Introduction

There is nothing so certain in life as death and taxes – and
Spain is no different in this respect from any other place.
This chapter is basically concerned with your tax liabilities as
a **home owner**. It does not go into great detail about the
complications of tax residence (although a limited
understanding is necessary, even for house purchase).

If you are thinking of moving permanently to Spain then it
would be very much in your interests to get good specialist
advice on the implications of residence on your tax position.
This should be done **before** you leave the UK.

The taxes that the home owner will be liable for in Spain fall
into two groups:

- The property taxes that are paid as a result of buying (or
  selling) a house.
- The annual taxes that are paid as a result of owning (and
  perhaps letting) a house.

In addition, there is inheritance tax to think about if you die.

There will also be differences (principally in relation to the
annual taxes) depending on whether you are resident or non-
resident for tax purposes and this is explained in more detail
in chapter 11.

What taxes might you have to pay?

The total list of taxes that you could be liable for looks rather daunting, but there are no particular surprises in it. There are a number of obvious ways in which you can be taxed as a home owner and, with the exception of wealth tax, the Spanish list is more or less identical to the UK list:

- If you buy a new home you will pay *IVA*, the Spanish equivalent of VAT (to the State). If you buy a second-hand house you will pay *ITP* (which is similar to *IVA*).
- When you buy any land, you may be liable for *plusvalia* (paid to the Town Hall).
- When you have paid for your home, you will be liable for rates (paid to the Town Hall) and *patrimonio* – wealth tax (paid to the State).
- If you let your home (and, if you are a non-resident, even if you **don't** let your home), you will have to pay *renta* – income tax (to the State).
- When you sell your home, you may pay *plusvalia* (to the Town Hall) and capital gains tax (to the State).
- If you transfer your home (either by gift or through your Will) you may pay *plusvalia* (to the Town Hall) and inheritance tax (to the State).

All these taxes are described in later sections of this chapter and in chapter 11.

The changing face of tax collection

Spain used to be a tax haven. This was not only because tax rates were low but also because the administration was somewhat inefficient. Tax evasion was a way of life and almost to be encouraged. This is no longer the case. Although some tax rates are still lower than their UK equivalent, others are more severe. Also the authorities are significantly more efficient than they used to be and now insist that you pay your dues.

In addition, the British practice of paying a tax bill some months after the tax return has been filled in is unheard of in Spain. The forms are designed to be filled in by the taxpayer or a representative and from the form it is possible to calculate your tax liability. Consequently, when you send in your forms, you send in your cheque at the same time. It's therefore important to be aware of the taxes that you are likely to meet in Spain.

We will look at taxes in two sections – the first section will be the taxes connected with the purchase and selling of the property and the second section (in chapter 11) will look at the personal taxes you have to pay as a result of owning (and perhaps letting) property in Spain. Chapter 11 will also look at inheritance tax.

Taxes on property

When you buy property in Spain, the two principal taxes that you must take into account are *IVA* (or *ITP*) and *plusvalia*. When you sell property you may face a liability to capital gains tax.

IVA

IVA is the Spanish equivalent of VAT and was introduced when Spain joined the Common Market on 1 January 1986. *IVA* is now applicable to many property transfers but not at the same rate for all kinds of property. In most cases, agricultural land (*finca rustica*) is exempt from *IVA* although you may have to pay a tax called *ITP*. The standard rate of *IVA* is 12%. Some luxuries are charged at 33% whereas some basic necessities are charged at only 6%.

IVA on buildings is only applicable if you are buying a new property from the developer or builder, not if you are buying a second-hand property from a private person. *IVA* is not charged on sales of second-hand property unless the seller is a person or company that habitually sells property, in which case you will pay *IVA* at 6%. If you buy a second-hand property from a private individual no *IVA* is levied – but you don't escape tax because *ITP* is charged.

The table shows the rates of *IVA* that are charged on the various types of building transactions that you might undertake:

Buying a building plot from a promoter	12%	*IVA*
Buying a plot and having a house constructed on it	6%	*IVA*
Buying commercial premises from a promoter	12%	*IVA*
Buying an apartment from a promoter	6%	*IVA*
Paying for extras on the construction	6%	*IVA*
Building a major extension eg a pool	12%	*IVA*
Paying for the '*Declaracion de Obra Nueva*'	0.5%	*IVA*

The varying rates are often the cause of confusion. Even the Spanish get confused and you may find yourself being charged 12% *IVA* when in fact 6% is the correct rate. The rules for the lower rate are as follows:

- The reduced rate of 6% applies if the building is basically for living in. A swimming pool is, therefore, not part of the dwelling but if it is constructed **at the same time** as the rest of the property, it will qualify for the lower rate. If it is added on at a later stage, then you will have to pay 12% – and this applies to any kind of extension.
- The reduced rate of 6% only applies if you are a party to the contract ie the contract is between you and the builder. If you arrange for **any** work to be done outside the contract (eg you find a cheap source of bathroom fittings and you pay for these yourself) you will pay *IVA* at 12% on the costs you have incurred yourself.
- If you buy an old house and contract with a builder for

modernisation work to be carried out, *IVA* at 6% will be charged provided the refurbishment costs are no less than 25% of the value of the house before renovation.

You will see that there is a particularly low rate of tax on what is called a *Declaracion de Obra Nueva* (Declaration of New Work). This is the tax on any new building work and this does give you an opportunity to reduce the tax on a new house being built on a building plot.

You arrange to buy the land first (and we will assume it is *finca urbana*) and complete all the legal details and pay the *IVA* at a rate of 12%. Having purchased the land, and got title to it, you can then arrange for the house to be built and pay *IVA* on the building construction at the rate of 0.5%. If you purchase the plot, arrange the construction with the builder and then pay the final amount over at the end of the construction period, then you will pay tax at 6% on the total cost.

It may, therefore, be cheaper to buy the land first, pay the tax and then put the building work in hand.

If you buy a *finca rustica*, then you will pay *ITP* at the rate of 6%. *ITP* at the rate of 6% is also charged on all purchases (plots, houses and flats) from a private owner.

The value on which tax is payable

Previously, part of the tax evasion in Spain was to declare a very small value in your title deed, often down to 10% of the market value. That in turn meant that you would pay a very small amount of tax on the purchase. This is now no longer possible because the tax authorities are giving notaries guidelines on what to accept. The authorities recognise that old practices die hard and so the declared values are gradually being pushed higher and higher each year closer to the realistic market value. At present, the declared value will represent approximately 70–80% of the market value (although there are a number of local variations) and it is this

value on which *IVA* is paid. But do take great care. The
authorities are very much stricter than they used to be and
understatement is not to be recommended.

You should of course note that the declared value should
correspond with the bank certificate – and that itself will
determine how much currency you can take out of Spain
when you come to sell the property. (See chapter 17 for
more details on selling your property).

There therefore appears to be an advantage in having a low
value in the title deeds because that reduces the tax bill.
However, when you finally sell the house, the difference
between the price you get and the original declared value
will be that much greater making it more difficult to export
the currency and also making you liable to a higher capital
gain, which is taxable.

This point cannot be stressed too strongly. It's one where you
may be advised by the 'old hands' to declare a low value
because that is the way things are done in Spain. They are
behind the times. For example, suppose you purchase a
property for 7m *pesetas* and declare 4m *pesetas* in order to
reduce the *IVA*:

- 4m *pesetas* will be on the bank certificate.
- The purchase price in the *escritura* is 4m *pesetas* as well.

In a few years time you might sell the property for, say, 14m
pesetas. The fiscal authorities will insist that you declare the
full price in the *escritura*. Not only would you have to pay
capital gains tax on 10m *pesetas*, you would be unable to
repatriate what was left of the 10m *pesetas*.

Plusvalia

Plusvalia is a **municipal** tax on the increase in value of land.
Because your property must lie on, or share, some land then
it's a tax which affects virtually every property in Spain.

Plusvalia is paid whenever the ownership of property changes (including inheritance under a Will) and this is important. Many properties have not changed hands for many years and will have accumulated a significant increase in value particularly over the last few years. Because of this, the maximum period over which the tax can be calculated is set at 30 years. Consequently, any action that involves a change of ownership (buying, selling, gifting or death) gives rise to a liability for *plusvalia*

One area where *plusvalia* is not levied is on land destined for agricultural purposes (*fincas rusticas*) as it applies only to building plots in towns and for land approved for development and construction. However, a number of people have bought *fincas rusticas* with the intention of building and with no intention of using it for agricultural purposes. In this case, it's something of a grey area so people with rural property shouldn't be too surprised if the Town Hall present them with a bill for *plusvalia*.

The levying of plusvalia

Plusvalia is levied and collected by the Town Hall. Each local authority has to register all properties in its area and the name of the owners, and make a continuous assessment of the land's value. This assessment has nothing to do with the value appearing in your title deeds – it will be increasingly closer to the real market value. The increase is publicised and so it's well worthwhile monitoring it.

If there is a house on the land, the Town Hall will make an estimate for both the value of the house and the value of the land, (because, as was pointed out before, *plusvalia* is a tax on the increase in the value of land, not the buildings). However, the land will always be at least 40% of the total value if the house is less than 10 years old and it will rise on a sliding scale to 80% if the house is over 75 years old.

The rates of plusvalia

It is the local authority who decide what has been the increase in the value of land on which the tax is being raised. They have tables which show them what the value is – or was – in any one year. The tables give different values for different areas and you will have to find out from the Town Hall what zone your property comes in so that you can look in the tables to make your own check. If you disagree then you raise the matter with the Town Hall.

The tables give values (in *pesetas* per square metre) showing the value of the land now and in all previous years. Provided you know the year in which the title last changed hands, you can work out the increase in value per square metre.

The increase in value is then expressed as a percentage of the **original** value and this percentage is then divided by the number of years that have elapsed since the title last changed hands. The result is the 'co-efficient' and it is this which determines the tax rate.

Value of co-efficient	Tax as percentage of increase in value
Less than 5	15%
5 – 10	17%
11 – 30	25%
31 – 50	35%
50+	40%

In other words, the maximum *plusvalia* is 40% of the 'official' increase in value of the land.

An example of plusvalia

In 1988, Mr A buys a small plot of land of 200 square metres from Mr B who bought it himself in 1978. The present value (according to index) is 8,000 *pesetas* per metre; the previous value in 1978 was 500 *pesetas* per metre. The increase in value since 1978 is therefore 7,500 *pesetas* per metre, ie 1,500,000 *pesetas*.

The percentage increase is the increase in value (7,500) divided by the previous value (500) multiplied by a hundred. The percentage increase is therefore 1,500%. This is then divided by ten (1978 to 1988) giving a co-efficient of 150. As this exceeds 50, the percentage of *plusvalia* is 40%.

The tax is therefore 40% of the increase in value. 40% of 1,500,000 *pesetas* is 600,000 *pesetas* and that is the amount the Town Hall will expect.

The above values are not particularly unrealistic given the rapid increase in the price of land over recent years. What it does point out is that the *plusvalia* can be quite a substantial amount of money and it's important to establish at the time of purchase exactly who's going to be responsible.

The payment of plusvalia

Plusvalia is the responsibility of the person selling the property. But it's common to have a clause in a purchase agreement saying that all taxes and costs that arise from the transfer of the property, including *plusvalia*, are to be paid by the buyer. Consequently, if you are buying property, you should find out when the last title deed for the property was made and what the *plusvalia* will amount to. The local authority can give you this information and your lawyer can offer you assistance.

Even if no agreement has been reached between the buyer and the seller, the buyer often ends up having to pay it anyway. The property itself is the means that the local authority possess to enforce payment. The property is in the buyer's hands, and, as the seller has frequently left the area, the buyer will have to foot the bill.

In practice, you will be advised to pay the tax after a transfer in the title of the property takes place and your final inscription as owner in the property register will be pending until the payment is made.

How to protect yourself

The best advice is to do two things:

1 Make sure you set aside enough money to pay the estimated percentage of the value increase if you think there is a chance that the seller will avoid his responsibility or if you have contracted to pay it.
2 Take the initiative to enquire at the Town Hall when it will be making the assessment so that you can be sure to avoid a surcharge.

Finally, if you have agreed with the seller that he will bear the cost of the *plusvalia*, the best way to ensure this is to agree with him that the tax will be deducted from the purchase price. You then have the funds available to pay yourself on demand and relieve the seller of the responsibility. You may find that some sellers are not too happy to accept such an arrangement but it's a worthwhile point to stand firm on if the *plusvalia* is going to be substantial.

The changes to plusvalia

At the end of December 1988, changes were announced in the way *plusvalia* is to be calculated in the future — the new rules will come into force on 1 January 1990. The changes are quite substantial although the basic principle of taxing the increase in the value of land is unchanged.

It is too early to provide a full explanation of the new rules in this edition of 'Your Home In Spain' as many of the details have yet to be announced. However, the Institute of Foreign Property Owners will be publishing details in its monthly magazine and the 1990 edition of 'Your Home In Spain' will contain a full explanation of the new tax.

Taxes to be paid on selling property

There are two taxes on the gain made on selling property:

1   The first of these is *plusvalia*, described earlier on.
2   The second tax is capital gains tax which is levied by the State and it differs according to whether you are a resident or a non-resident of Spain (see next chapter).

Capital gains tax on sales by non-residents

The assessment of your capital gain is straightforward. The Inland Revenue will levy the current rate of tax (which in 1987 was 20% but was raised to 35% in 1988) on the gain which is the difference between the declared values (ie the value in the *escritura*) at the beginning and end of your ownership. Many non-resident foreigners have sold their properties in foreign currency outside Spain but this does not remove your obligation to declare this tax through your fiscal representative. Also, you are obliged to declare the sale on your UK tax return and you could be liable to UK capital gains tax in that way.

Capital gains tax on sales by residents

This is rather more complicated because your capital gains are tied up with your income tax declaration. Consequently, the capital gain that you make as a resident when you sell your property is classed as income for the year in which it was sold. The total gain you make is reduced slightly by an indexation allowance (which your tax adviser will calculate) and is then divided by the number of years you have been in possession of the property. The result is then added to your other income for the year in question to determine the total tax that you pay.

Once again, don't think that you can reduce the tax by making low declarations of value. There are cases in which the Spanish Inland Revenue has not accepted a valuation which even a notary has allowed and has made its own higher valuation accompanied by a supplementary tax bill. It's worth noting that the Inland Revenue can intervene in this way at any time during the two years after the sale and the easiest way to avoid this kind of unpleasant surprise is to agree with the buyer to declare the full value of the property when making the transfer.

If you sell your home and buy another property as your principal residence within two years, you may be relieved of capital gains tax altogether provided the property you are selling has an *escritura* value of less than 15m *pesetas* (or an allowance may be made for it in a subsequent declaration if it has already been paid). But make sure you get the timing right. Sell the mansion, **then** buy the cottage! If you own both at once, for however short a time, you are regarded as having increased your wealth and will be taxed accordingly without any reliefs. The date of the transaction is the date when you make the *escritura*.

If you are selling your property with a view to returning to the UK then you should get specialist advice as your return should be carefully timed to minimise your tax liabilities.

11 The tax system – Part 2

The annual taxes

Spain has two principal forms of annual taxation – wealth tax and income tax and most people regardless of whether they are resident in Spain or not will have to make some kind of tax declaration every year.

Appointing a fiscal representative

One very important point for non-residents is that you are **obliged** to appoint a fiscal representative in Spain and there is growing pressure from the Spanish government to make sure that you do. It must be done in a letter to your local Ministry of Finance but the representative can be for example, a Spaniard, a *gestor*, a foreigner, a company or a private person. *Gestors* have no equivalent in Britain: they arise from the bureaucracy of the Spanish Civil Service – they are in effect professional form fillers. They are aware of the system to be followed and they know which form is required, how it's completed, how many copies are needed and where to send it. They will have virtually everything you need from applying for a driving licence to the filling in of a tax return. In the Appendix is a sample letter appointing a fiscal representative.

Alternatively you can appoint an *asesor fiscal* to look after your affairs. He or she is the equivalent of an accountant and will have an excellent understanding of the tax regulations and will be able to help you with ways of perhaps reducing your tax liability.

Everybody who has any kind of financial interest in Spain (and this includes the property owner) should have a fiscal identification number. Your fiscal representative may be able to help you obtain one.

The deadline for filing personal income and wealth tax returns is early June as the period during which the forms must be sent in to the authorities is from 1 May to 20 June. The Spanish tax year is the calendar year and so the returns will assess your income during the previous year and assess your wealth as at 31 December.

A word of advice on becoming a fiscal representative yourself. The tax authorities are now putting pressure on them, and, in some cases, fining them for non-payment of taxes by their clients. If you are asked to act as a fiscal representative on behalf of a friend, think carefully before saying 'yes'.

Resident or non-resident?

First though, let us clear up the business about whether you are resident or non-resident and remember it is important to distinguish between **tax** status and **immigration** status. This chapter deals solely with residence for tax purposes; immigration status is covered in chapter 18.

Most countries in the world have broadly similar rules for determining tax residence, but we will start by looking at the UK regulations. You will be regarded as tax resident in the UK if:

- You spend 183 days or more per annum in the UK.
- You make habitual and substantial visits to the UK – visits are treated as habitual if they are made each year

for four consecutive years and substantial if they last an average of three months (90 days or more) per annum when measured over that period.
- You make a visit to the UK, no matter how short the duration, and you have accommodation available for your use.

This latter point would appear to be a total catch-all but in fact it is waived for people in full-time gainful employment abroad. Nevertheless, it is an important consideration for the retired person.

Turning now to the Spanish rules; you will be tax resident in Spain in any year that you spend more than six months there, and once again six months is defined as 183 days or more. Residence applies to the whole family unit – husband, wife and children under eighteen. What this means is that if one member of the family is resident for tax purposes, the other members will also be regarded as tax resident as well.

In computing the period of residence, absences are not taken into account unless the circumstances suggest that they will be for more than three years. This means that, if you leave Spain, then unless it is clear that you will not be returning for at least three years, you will continue to be treated as a tax resident during your absence.

In both the UK and Spanish residence rules 'year' means the tax year. However, in the UK, the tax year runs from 6 April to 5 April whereas in Spain (as in most other countries of the world) the tax year is the same as the calendar year. The slightly different rules and periods means that it is perfectly possible for someone to be tax resident in both countries at once. This is not quite as bad as it sounds as there is a Double Taxation Agreement in force between Spain and the UK which ensures, in essence, that tax is not levied twice on the same income. However, you should always bear in mind that these agreements also exist to make sure that you are taxed at least once!

The overall result for most people is that their tax status is determined by whether or not they have accommodation available to them in the UK or by the number of days a year they spend either in the UK or in Spain. Immigration status (as explained in chapter 18) is determined by whether or not the Spanish authorities are prepared to grant you residence status – they will take their taxes off you whether they like you or not! However they are now getting more insistent that if you stay in Spain for more than 182 days (ie you become tax resident) you must also apply for your *residencia*.

This chapter deals principally with the non-resident property owner although, where appropriate, it touches on the physical considerations for the resident property owner. In this case, the comments should be regarded as a guide and no substitute for specialist advice.

One particular area (which is beyond the scope of this book) is for people leaving England permanently to live in Spain. The precise day on which you leave the UK can have a significant impact on your tax bill and it's vital to take professional advice on that.

The new proposals

The UK rules described above relate to Inland Revenue law and practice as at December 1988 but it should be noted that this is currently under review. The Revenue issued a consultative document in July 1988 (Residents in the United Kingdom – the Scope of UK Taxation for Individuals) proposing a radical overhaul of the rules relating to the taxation of both Britons abroad and foreign nationals in the UK.

The proposals are complex and, of course, at this stage are just proposals – there is no indication of which proposals will be enacted or when. However, it is worth pointing out that the envisaged changes would be beneficial to British expatriates retired abroad. In effect, the amount of time that could be spent in the UK without becoming tax resident would be increased from an average of 90 days per annum to 120 days per annum and, more importantly, the 'visits with accommodation available' rule would be scrapped, thus enabling a Briton to keep a home in the UK without prejudicing his tax position.

This is good news, of course, but, for the time being, the prudent individual will organise his affairs in accordance with current legislation – whilst perhaps looking expectantly to the future.

Annual taxes you will have to pay

The main annual taxes that affect people with property in Spain are as follows:

- Wealth tax.
- Property taxes.
- Income tax.

Wealth tax

If you are **non-resident** in Spain, then you must pay wealth tax (the *patrimonio*) on all your assets situated in Spain. Assets include your house, bank accounts and other assets with a determined value (eg stocks and shares). The value of your house is the official estimate that appears in your receipt for local rates and it is called the *valor catastral*. (If you are not yet registered as a rate payer then the value used will be the declared value in the *escritura*). Wealth tax has to be paid each year but it is a low tax (about 0.2% of the total value of your assets for most people). However, it must be paid in order to prevent any problems when you come to sell your property.

For **residents**, the tax rates are the same but apply to your **worldwide** assets. The tax only applies if your assets exceed 4m *pesetas*. However, there are allowances of 9m *pesetas* for a single person and 12m *pesetas* for a married couple (with increases of 1.5 million *pesetas* for each child under the age of 25).

Property taxes

Spain has a rates system called the *Contribucion Territorial Urbana* (or the *Contribucion Territorial Rustica* if you live in a *finca rustica*). Every owner has to pay property taxes and it's up to you to check your liability for payment with the local Town Hall. Unfortunately the Town Hall won't write and tell you.

The amount of tax you have to pay is based on your rateable value, the *valor catastral* (ie the same value that you have to show on your wealth tax return). In addition to the basic rates, you may also find that your local Town Hall will introduce local taxes and charges (*tasas*) from time to time to pay for local developments and services. Also, you may find these charges built into the rates for garbage collection etc.

A particular tax to look out for is called the *Contribuciones Especiales*. This is a local tax on the benefit or increase in the value of your property caused by any public works or installations carried out by the local authorities.

The Town Hall can allocate 90% of the cost of the work in the form of this special tax on the owners of whatever property they believe has benefited from the work being carried out. If a number of properties are affected, the tax will be distributed amongst the properties based on the length of the road frontage of the plot, the size of the plot, the volume of the building and the value of your property. The tax is payable when the work has been finished or the new sevice implemented but it can also be demanded in part payments as the work progresses.

The Town Hall are obliged to notify each owner about this tax but if they don't have your address in the UK, then the information will be published in the official Town Hall Bulletin.

The simplest solution to paying your rates is to make an arrangement with your bank for them to pay the taxes on your behalf. Once you have established with the Town Hall that you are going to pay the taxes, you can then send the necessary forms to your bank and they will pay the taxes on your behalf.

Another point to make is that property taxes are starting to rise with some very sharp increases in some areas. This is due not only to the local Town Hall increasing the *valor catastral* on individual properties but also by the percentages applied to this value which the Government is allowing to rise from the previous limit of 20% to up to 40% under certain conditions.

From 1 January 1990, both the *Contribucion Urbana* and the *Contribucion Rustica* will disappear and be replaced by a new property tax (called the *Impuesto sobre bienes muebles*). It will continue to be expressed as a percentage of the *valor catastral*.

Income tax

You are liable to income tax (*renta*) – which is applied at a minimum rate of 25% – in the following ways:

- If you are tax resident in Spain then you are liable to tax on your worldwide income (including Spanish capital gains) in excess of 840,000 *pesetas* whether it is sent to you in Spain or not. Against this, there are a range of reliefs that you may deduct, followed by a range of allowances. If your total income doesn't exceed 840,000 *pesetas* then there is no need for you to make any tax return at all, though you will need to submit a 'nil-return' if you are renewing your *residencia*.

- If you are non-resident in Spain, you are taxed on any income arising from a source within Spain, such as your income from letting your property (and this includes any income paid to you in the UK or elsewhere as well).

There's also a rather unusual part of Spanish law which requires everybody to include 2% of the rateable value of their property as a notional rental income paid by themselves to themselves. People who are resident for tax purposes in Spain have several allowances in their income tax return and this will reduce the impact of this particular tax.

If you are a non-resident, you will be liable to tax at a minimum rate of 20% on 2% of the *valor catastral* regardless of whether you are letting your property or not.

As an example, if you are the non-resident owner of an apartment in Spain with a *valor catastral* of 2m *pesetas*, you will be liable to tax at 20% on 2% of this value (ie 20% of 40,000 *pesetas*, a tax bill of 8,000 *pesetas*).

If you **do** let your property, then you will of course be liable to tax on the income you receive. However, the notional tax described above is reduced accordingly ie if you let your property for three months of the year, the notional rental income is assessed at only 9/12 of 2% of the *valor catastral*. The Spanish authorities are increasing the pressure on property owners to pay this tax. There is now a special form (Form 210) for the payment of the tax and the form has to be signed by your fiscal representative.

Inheritance tax

Inheritance tax is a tax that you must take into account, especially if you intend to live in Spain. It does, however, apply to non-residents as well. Inheritance tax arises if you give assets away while you are alive or if you leave them to somebody in your Will. It is therefore similar to UK inheritance tax but it is much more severe in the impact it can have, particularly for the wealthy.

Who is liable to pay it?

- Inheritance tax is levied on the person receiving or inheriting the assets (the beneficiary).
- If you are resident in Spain, then you are liable to inheritance tax on any assets given or bequeathed to you regardless of where they are situated.
- If you are non-resident then you are liable to Spanish inheritance tax if you are given or are bequeathed assets that are situated in Spain (and an obvious example is a house or apartment).

How is it calculated?

The calculation of the tax is complex but it is simple to follow in stages; the liability to inheritance tax is based on:

- The relationship between the giver and the receiver.
- The value of the gift or property.
- The existing wealth of the receiver (ie total wealth if you are resident, Spanish wealth if you are non-resident).

By way of simple illustration, take the case of a retired couple of relatively modest means living in Spain. If the husband dies, his widow could well have a small inheritance tax bill to pay. If, however, a wealthy widow were to leave her estate to her equally wealthy next door neighbour, the neighbour could face a substantial tax bill.

The relationship

There are four groups of relationship of the person receiving the gift:

Group I	–	children and grandchildren under 21 (including adopted children).
Group II	–	other children and grandchildren, spouse, parents and grandparents.
Group III	–	other close relations (eg brothers and sisters)
Group IV	–	first cousins and other more distant relatives, and non-relatives (which includes common law spouses).

The value

The new law on inheritance tax that took effect from 1 January 1988 stresses that the value of the inheritance or gift is the real value, ie the market value. For most people, the major asset will be their home and the value of the home will be the value for *plusvalia* and the current market price for similar properties. The value of the gift may be **reduced** by certain allowances of up to 6.0m *pesetas* according to the relationship group:

Group I	–	2m *ptas* + 0.5m *ptas* for each year below 21
Group II	–	2m *ptas*
Group III	–	1m *ptas*
Group IV	–	Nil

Existing wealth

The rate of tax is 7.65% on small gifts of up to 1m *pesetas* rising in bands to a rate of 16.15% on values in excess of 10m *pesetas*. For larger gifts in excess of 15m *pesetas* the rate

rises progressively until it reaches a top rate of 34% on gifts
in excess of 100m *pesetas*.

The tax rate is then multiplied by a co-efficient (ranging from
1 to 2.4) which depends on the relationship and the existing
wealth of the recipient **before** adding in the gift:

Existing wealth (million *pesetas*)	Group I,II	Group III	Group IV
0 – 50	1	1.5882	2
50+ – 250	1.05	1.6676	2.1
250+ – 500	1.1	1.7471	2.2
500+	1.2	1.9059	2.4

The overall result is that on gifts of less than 2m *pesetas*
between close relatives there will be no tax at all to pay
(because of the allowances); on substantial gifts between
friends the tax rate could be as high as just over 80% (ie
34% × 2.4).

Example

Mr B, who is retired, owns a villa with an estimated value of 10m
pesetas. He dies and leaves it to his wife who has no other assets in
Spain.

Calculation

1   The relationship is Group II which carries an allowance of 2m
    pesetas.
2   The value of the gift is 5m *pesetas* (because in Spanish law,
    husband and wife have joint ownership of property) reduced to
    a taxable value of 3m because of the allowance.
3   The tax rate on a gift of 3m *pesetas* is 8.5%.
4   Mrs B's total wealth is less than 50m *pesetas* which means a co-
    efficient of 1.00.
5   The tax due is therefore 8.5% of 3m *pesetas* which means a bill
    of 255,000 *pesetas*.

Gifting property

Inheritance tax therefore is an important tax and you should always take into account that if you give your property away either when you are alive or when you die, the person who receives the property could have a sizeable tax bill.

In the UK it is possible to give property to your wife free of UK inheritance tax and to make limited gifts to your children in a way which may avoid inheritance tax. **No such provisions exist in Spain**. However, there is one way in which inheritance tax can be reduced and that is by using what is called the *usufructo*. This is how it works.

When buying a property in Spain you can make a split in the *escritura* between *el nudo propiedad* (the bequeathed property) and the *usufructo* (the user's rights). You can insert your children (or grandchildren) as the real owners of the property, but reserve the use of the property for the lifetime of yourself and your spouse, or for a specified period of time.

If you die, the inheritance tax is based on the unexpired use of the property.

(a)   If you reserve the user's right for yourself for a certain time, expressed in years, and you subsequently die before the stipulated time has passed, your heirs will have to pay inheritance tax on the user's right remaining. This will be calculated at the rate of 2% of the total value of the property for each year remaining, up to a maximum of 70%.

(b)   If you reserve for yourself the user's right for life, the value of the user's right is fixed at 70% of the total value of the property, reduced by 1% per year for each year that you survive beyond the age of 20.

For example, if you died at age 70, you would have survived for 50 years beyond the age of 20 which would mean that the percentage would be reduced by 50% ie a net rate of 20%.

If you had died at age 80, you would have survived for 60 years beyond the age of 20 and the 70% would reduce down to 10%.

The way you plan your investments and prepare things in the event of your death is closely tied up with the way you write your Will. It is absolutely essential to write a Spanish Will if you have property in Spain and this is dealt with in more detail in chapter 20.

One thing is **absolutely** clear and that is that if you are planning to retire to Spain you need to think very carefully indeed about the potential impact of Spanish inheritance tax and take competent financial advice.

'Offshore' companies

Given the range of taxation which can have an impact on the property owner in Spain, the use of offshore companies or trusts (or a combination of both) is growing. The basic reasoning behind this arrangement is that such devices can protect assets by paying as little tax as possible and by being able to transfer or sell the property, again without any tax liability. This approach is quite legal and the ownership of property in Spain through such a device is often used to avoid the payment of some taxes but not all.

The basic principle is that a company, with nominated shareholders, is set up outside Spain to buy property inside Spain. Taxes will be paid by the company in the usual way when buying the property in the first place. Thereafter, the tax position changes because on all subsequent buying and selling of the property, the ownership of the property does not change. The property is still owned by the company; it is the ownership of the company that is bought and sold.

The establishment of a suitable company outside Spain can be arranged in the Isle of Man, the Channel Islands and even the UK. However, it is **strongly** recommended that you take professional advice before undertaking this kind of transaction. The current position is very much dependent on the way the Spanish authorities will regard the establishment of offshore companies and there is no guarantee that legislation will not be introduced in the future to wipe out all the tax benefits. Like any other government, the Spanish Government does not like people enjoying the benefits of living in Spain but avoiding all their tax obligations.

In very broad terms, the only time that the purchase of a property in Spain through a foreign company can be justified is by those people who would otherwise find themselves in an essentially unfair tax situation. These would typically be elderly persons buying a very valuable property which could mean that their heirs fell into tax categories where inheritance tax at the rate of more than 50% could be charged. By and large, the method would only be recommended if the investment was over 20m *pesetas*.

12 Things to bear in mind

Whether you are buying a second-hand property, a new house or having a house built, there are a number of points you have to bear in mind. Often, these would not occur to you at home. Here, used to water on tap, it would never occur to ask if it is salty or not. So this chapter is to alert you to some of the things that you might not have taken into account at the start of your house buying search.

The extras when buying

People have often had nasty shocks when buying because they have not been told about the extras that can – and often do – occur. In some extreme cases, the extras can often add up to more than the purchase price of the property.

The additional cost depends on what sort of property you buy, how you buy it and from whom. If you buy an old farmhouse the conversion costs could be higher than the purchasing price (and also higher than the seller's estimate). If you buy a new home, you might find that you've got some construction work to do on the garden that hadn't been taken into account. If you buy a second-hand house, you might find that you have to replace the sanitary system or perhaps do some repairs to the roof.

Commissions and taxes

If you are buying a second-hand property and decided to use the services of a real estate agent, it's better to check first to find out what the position is with commission. If you are not careful, you might be asked to pay part of his commission – often up to as much as 5% of the property value. Always ask to have the position clarified before purchasing and, to be on the safe side, get it in writing.

Whatever you buy, you will have some legal fees to pay for the official registration of the property. You will also have to pay the Spanish equivalent of VAT on your purchase and there will also be a tax due on the increase in value of the land since it last changed hands. This is called *plusvalia* and this would normally be paid by the person selling the house but if you are contracting with him, then make sure that it's put in writing that he will pay and not you. The tax position is explained in more detail in chapter 10.

The services

Regardless of the type of property that you are buying, there are certain areas that you need to watch carefully, some of them rather different from those you are used to when buying property in the UK.

Paying for services

In some cases, you may have to pay for the connection of services. Electricity meters, for example, must be installed in your name by the local electricity company. If you are having to get a new connection made from the local supply, together with meter installation, you might find you are paying quite a sizeable sum of money. If you plan to have a telephone, check carefully with the telephone company on the costs of installation. If you are in a particularly isolated area, it could cost thousands of pounds. Check before you commit yourself. Find out the position with water. In some areas, the water distribution is the responsibility of a private company and you might find you are having to pay quite a sizeable sum of money for connection to the supply.

Water

Although Spain has a fairly substantial rainfall, it doesn't fall evenly over Spain and the rain that does fall is not particularly well harnessed. Consequently, there is surplus rainfall in the north and a scarcity along the Mediterranean coast and in the Balearic Islands. Moreover, the rain tends to come in short periods (towards the end of the Autumn) occasionally creating floods which are sometimes devastating. Not only that, Spain is now required to share its water with some 25 million tourists who come to visit Spain (usually in the driest period of the year!). In addition to this there is the increasing volume of residential development on the Mediterranean coastline.

Because of this, it's very advisable to look into the water situation in the area where you intend to buy. Not surprisingly, the people selling property aren't too keen to talk about it so make a point of asking your prospective new neighbours what the problems are. Above all, be prepared to pay for your water – most houses have a water meter and you will pay for it in much the same way as you pay for electricity. This means a standing charge plus a variable charge depending on the amount of water that you use.

Make sure you understand what the tariffs are in advance. In some cases, you may find that you have to pay a rental charge to the water company regardless of whether you are actually using water or not. That's not necessarily a discrimination against the foreigner – the increased tariff often applies to second homes and, as one Spanish family in 13 owns a second home, it's something that they complain about as well.

In the Appendix you will find an example of how to read a water bill.

Sweet or sour?

In some areas near the coast, you may find that water is being drawn from a very low water table which means that at peak times in the year, the water turns salty. Under those circumstances, you are going to have to rely on bottled water from the local supermarket or go to the expense of building a *deposito* which is a sort of large water storage tank. You will need planning permission in order to build one of these but, before you do, make sure there is a local supply that is readily accessible to you. Water lorries are not a familiar sight in Britain – they are in Spain.

Electricity

In a correctly built urbanisation, the electricity supply will be to the edge of your plot. In the price of the construction for the house you should ensure that the electricity connection is included. You should only have to pay for the contract with the electricity company and for the meter.

The contract with the electricity company must be made in the name of the owner and to get the contract you must have the certificate from the installer of the wiring. As we said earlier, make sure that you get this certificate otherwise you won't be able to connect electricity to your house.

Paying for your electricity

Normally, the reading of your meter will take place every two months. Some companies have the right to make an estimate of the consumption every second time without actually reading the meter. This will then be marked on your electricity bill as an estimate with a correcting reading being taken on the next occasion. It's worth bearing in mind that occasionally, this estimate tends to be a rather large one ie you end up financing the electricity company for six months of the year. If your average electricity usage is £30 every two months, you might find yourself paying £50 for one two-month period followed by a 'corrected' charge of £10 for the next.

The simplest way to pay for your electricity is through your bank, via standing order (and you will find details on how to set this up in chapter 9). The electricity board will take the money from your bank account and will then send you a copy of the meter reading to explain why they charged you what they have. This will then save any problems with missed payments although the electricity companies don't have the right to cut off your supply without notice if you don't pay the bill. What they will do is to send you a certified letter asking you to pay – but this goes to your address in Spain and if you are not there, there's little you can do about it.

In the Appendix there's a section on how to read your electricity bill.

The telephone

There is one aspect to life in Spain which you have to get used to very early on and that concerns the telephone system. Throughout Spain, the use of public telephone boxes is very widespread and they are very easy to use and very efficient. When it comes to having a telephone installed in your own home, things are very different.

The telephone company in Spain is a public company under the supervision of the Government. In each province the company has a delegation and they are the people to contact when you wish to install a phone. All you have to do is to phone the appropriate number, state that you wish to have a phone installed and they will take a note of your name and address. They will then write to you telling you whether you can have a phone or not and, if you can, the price and the contract conditions. You sign the contract if you agree to pay the price they are quoting and return it to the company. You then sit back and wait for the installation men to come. And wait.

Occasionally, you can be lucky and get a phone installed quickly. In other areas, all the lines are taken and you will wait months if not years for a telephone to be installed.

The cost of installation

Under normal circumstances, you will pay an installation fee of £60 for the line and a small sum for the phone you've chosen. You will be offered various models of phones and connections – if you don't have any particular needs just order a straightforward line and the simplest model you can. This will save you money both in the installation and on the bi-monthly phone bills. When you get a phone, you have the right to receive the telephone directory free of charge. (Even if you don't have a phone then it can be advisable to buy a directory because you will find it filled with valuable information.)

If you've chosen the cheapest form of line and telephone, the monthly standing charge will be about £4 or £5. If you are over 64 years old or are handicapped and living on a reduced income, then you can apply to the telephone company for a reduced standing charge; if you are successful, then the charge will only be about 40p or 50p a month.

The sewerage

Although it's a slightly indelicate subject, do make sure you enquire about the sewage disposal arrangements. Mains sewerage is not particularly common on some of the newer developments on the coastal regions but in most cases you will find that your property is connected to a cesspool without any particular problems. Do find out what the arrangements are for the emptying of the cesspool because in some cases you might find that there is a special tax levied by the local municipality to cover this particular problem.

What is important is that you find out where the cesspool covers are because they often require emptying so infrequently that they get covered over, and, most unfortunate of all, occasionally built over by such things as paths or terraces. It's a simple thing to overlook.

Criminality

Those people who came to Spain in the early 70s are sure to remember that you could leave your house unlocked or leave your car open on the street all night. Unfortunately, Spain is like every other country in Western Europe and has seen a significant increase in crime against property. Although part of the problem can be put down to unemployment in some areas, it's also an unfortunate reflection of increasing drug abuse. In the last few years, the amount of crime resulting from drugs and the relentless trafficking of drugs along the coasts has been on the increase.

This is something which the property owner cannot afford to ignore and it's a fact that must be taken into consideration when deciding where and what property to buy. If you are not going to be living permanently in your home, or if you are going to live there alone, you should be careful when buying in an isolated location. Many isolated houses are broken into during the owner's long absences and even while they are staying in them. If you are going to be away for long periods, it makes sense to buy a house in an area where someone can keep a watchful eye on it.

Be on your guard

It's often the case that break-ins and robberies of holiday homes happen when the property is occupied but when the family have just gone out for a while to the shops or to a restaurant. Criminals seem to expect that there will be money in the house when people are living there. And it is cash, or valuables that can be turned into cash, they are after. Your furniture and clothes are normally of little interest.

Break-ins also often occur as soon as people arrive on holiday. It's at that time that you have a fair amount of cash on you and it's also at a time when you are least on your guard. So, as a tip, take extra special care when you first arrive in Spain on holiday. Lock your valuables and cash away and make sure that all the doors and windows are locked when you go out for that first restaurant meal.

Home security

When buying your home or having one built, it makes sense to think about its security. One of the simplest solutions (and a common one in Spain) is to have metal grilles across all the windows and also to have special metal grille doors as well as wooden doors. Wherever possible, have double locks for additional security and make sure that all the windows can be well secured from inside the house.

Install a safe

It could be well worth your while to install a safe somewhere inside the house. If you are using your home for a holiday, you are going to have to bring passports with you, credit cards, tickets, cash, travellers cheques and so on and it can be a problem keeping all this secure if you don't have the correct facilities. Installing a safe isn't very difficult and it can save a lot of unnecessary carrying around of valuables if you install one. Think carefully about the jewellery you take on holiday – it's far easier to leave it at home in the security of your own bank and it isn't absolutely essential to take your best watch and rings with you if all you are looking for is three weeks in the sun.

Insuring your property

Like all property, you must insure your home and the contents as well. It's occasionally difficult to get an insurance company in this country to insure your property abroad especially if it's being used primarily for holidays. You might find that your own insurance company is more sympathetic but their reluctance is because holiday homes are often left unoccupied for large parts of the year leading to more claims for damage and theft.

You will generally find it slightly more expensive to insure a holiday home abroad and you might find that some of the cover is restricted (for example theft or burst pipes) if the house is left unoccupied for extended periods of time. With some contents cover, you might even find that theft (one of the biggest risks) is excluded entirely so read the small print carefully.

The location of your property will also affect how the policy is taken out. Most of the larger British insurance companies will have offices or agencies in most Western European countries. That's important with Spain because insurance policies must be issued in Spain and in Spanish. Insurance, therefore, can be arranged in Britain, but it will be issued through the company's office in Spain.

If your property is in a rural area (ie somewhat isolated) you may find that difficult to insure in the UK. What insurers prefer to deal with is property in locations they are familiar with so you may have to make arrangements with a local insurer.

If you are taking your valuables or money abroad with you, then check carefully with your home insurance company to see exactly what type of insurance you are covered for. It's best to have an 'all risks' policy but do bear in mind that an all risks policy will cover you for accidental loss – it won't cover you if you've been deliberately careless. If your camera is stolen then you are covered – if your camera is stolen because you've left it on a crowded beach whilst you go for a swim, then don't expect your insurance company to be too sympathetic.

Do take care when making a claim as your insurance company will require a certificate from the police before settling a claim resulting from criminal activity. You must tell the police the value of everything that you have lost and they will write it into the certificate. You must be ready with these figures before you go and see the police.

Running costs and maintenance

One thing you shouldn't ignore when buying property in Spain is the running costs. These can add up to quite significant amounts and it's something you can take account of in advance:

- There will be standing charges on electricity, telephone and water whether you use the services or not. The cost of electricity is rising rapidly.
- Local property rates and other municipal charges could be between £50 and £100 for an average property.
- Some local authorities have not reassessed their rates for many years and are about to. You may still pay less than you are accustomed to – but it's beginning to become an item that you can't ignore.
- If you live in an urbanisation with community fees, or in an apartment block, then you will have annual charges

to pay which could be as low as £200 a year or could be over £500 a year.

● If you have your own plot with a swimming pool and garden, then you will have maintenance costs to pay for both.

The costs of maintenance

Over and above the running costs, you have to consider the maintenance costs of the property itself. Don't believe that just because you have a home in the sun, it won't require maintenance. The rain in Spain may fall infrequently but, when it does, it can be almost tropical. Those white houses look lovely in the sunshine – but they soon get dirty and start to look shabby. They're going to need re-painting about once every three years.

Those grilles and railings may look absolutely magnificent when they're first painted, but the influence of the Spanish sun and possibly a sea breeze or two will soon have that black paint looking less than sparkling. You are going to have to keep your property in good repair and that's something that you may not have thought about. If your property is being used principally for holidays, you don't necessarily want to spend half your holidays with the paintbrush in your hand and although Spain may have been cheap in the past, you could well find that painters and decorators are just as expensive in Spain as in the UK.

13 Renting and timeshare as an alternative

If you come to Spain and have a thoroughly enjoyable two weeks' holiday, then that can be a very good reason for coming to Spain again and having another thoroughly enjoyable fortnight. However, an annual two week holiday isn't a good reason for going through all the problems of buying a property.

So, an early decision has to be whether or not buying property is really worthwhile. The annual cost of even a small property in Spain (including the interest you lose on the money you have used to purchase the property) will almost certainly be more than the cost of a two week holiday. If you only need your own property for the freedom that it gives you, then renting a property could be a far cheaper option. Many of the major tour operators now provide villa holidays and there are a number of specialist organisations which have grown up purely to organise villa rental.

If, on the other hand, you can get out to Spain two or three times a year or if other members of your family can put it to good use when you don't need it, then the idea of a second home might look a lot more attractive. And there's no doubt that having a familiar base in Spain where you can 'do your own thing' is for many people the starting point for an ideal holiday.

Timesharing

Timesharing is another alternative to outright property purchase. The principle of timesharing is simple enough:

- A developer builds a number of units in a single development which could be a series of individual houses or a block of apartments.
- Rather than buy a unit outright, you purchase the right to use the property for a specified period each year for a specified number of years.
- The right of use is an asset which you can sell or temporarily exchange for a similar right in another property even in another country. You may also let other people use the property if you are unable to use it yourself during your particular time period.
- All the annual costs of running the complete property are paid for by a management company, set up by the developer, and you will be charged an annual management fee to cover all these costs.

In principle, therefore, timesharing is a relatively inexpensive way of purchasing a share in a property with exclusive rights to use it at a given time. Some people use this principle to vary their holidays throughout the year and buy timeshares in two or three properties. It can be a very effective method of providing yourself with a holiday base without the overall problems of actually owning a property.

The pressure to buy

However, like everything in life, it's not entirely without its problems. The first of these is a simple matter of mathematics. By selling the future use of a property, the developer recovers his initial cost very quickly and makes a tidy profit as well. He retains the ownership of the overall property itself so he has both sold it and kept it. All the future costs of running the property are taken care of by the management fee and the end result is a rather lucrative business for the developer. All you then need is for a number of developers to realise the potential of timesharing and you have the ideal breeding ground for problems. The lure of a home in the sun to the buyer with a prospect of quick profits to the seller leads immediately to the formation of a high pressure sales team with the end result that timesharing – and the timesharing companies – now have a dreadful reputation in Spain and Portugal.

Holidaymakers, particularly on the Costa del Sol and the Canary Islands, have been literally plagued by timeshare salespeople who have pestered them to attend timeshare exhibitions. Once there, the pressure to commit yourself to the purchase of a two week timeshare is intense with all kinds of inducements being offered to would-be purchasers. The position has got so bad that the Office of Fair Trading in London has produced a series of guidelines to people contemplating buying a timeshare:

- Sign nothing during your first meeting with the salesman unless you are given a written guarantee that you have the right to change your mind within a reasonable period of time.
- Pay nothing, not even a small deposit, at the first meeting unless you're completely sure you want to go ahead (and unless the deposit is refundable if you change your mind within a reasonable period of time).
- Beware of any pressure put on you to sign at once to obtain a discount or other benefit.
- Beware of gifts and prizes which may be designed to encourage you to visit the site or to buy within a deadline.
- Insist on full details in writing of what you're being offered. These details should include:
  - The full price.
  - The type of tenure you will have.
  - How you are to pay for it (including interest rates).
  - A copy of the contract.

- — Any additional terms or conditions.
- — Information on what will happen at the end of the timeshare.

- Take your time considering the offer. You should read the contract and get independent advice from your solicitor in the UK.

- Ask about maintenance charges. They're likely to go up after you have bought so check what is planned, what the charges include and how the increases are to be decided and by whom.

- Find out if there is an owner's association to represent your interests. You should find out what power they have over the management company and what say you will have in the management arrangements.

- Finally, make sure you really can afford what you are about to buy and don't think of a timeshare as an investment in the same way as buying a house or flat as your permanent home.

There are, of course, a number of perfectly ethical developers in the timeshare market. They have been seriously troubled by the tactics that have been used by other companies and they have formed the Timeshare Developers Association.

Members of the Association operate a five day cooling-off period and are obliged to follow the requirements of a code of conduct. The Association has also produced its own leaflet (available from the Association's offices at 23, Buckingham Gate, London SW1E 6LB telephone 01–921 8845) which highlights some questions you should ask:

- Is the timeshare part of an exchange organisation?
- Is there a cooling-off period?
- Are there any penalties if you decide not to go ahead?
- Is there an association of names?

Perhaps the most important advice they give you is to regard a timeshare as an investment in **holidays** and not to regard it as an investment in property.

The legal position

Part of the problem for timeshare in Spain is that whilst the law is able to recognise the division of an apartment block into various units (which is why you can buy the legal title to an apartment) it is not able to recognise the further subdivision of the ownership of that apartment into periods of time (which is why you cannot buy the **legal title** to two week's use of that apartment). This is the major difference between Spanish and Portuguese law as the law in Portugal **does** give you legal rights to the ownership of property for a stated period of time.

Consequently in Spain, your legal position with a timeshare is not very strong.

So what should you be aware of when entering into a timeshare agreement? The most important points to take note of are:

- Exactly what rights are you buying?
- What will happen in the future?

As a first step, you must make sure you fully understand the details of what you are buying. The following checklist is by no means exhaustive but it will give you an idea of the sort of thing to look out for in the purchasing contract:

- Who actually owns the property?
- Is the time period guaranteed?
- Can you let other people use the property?
- Can you sub-let the property?
- Are there any restrictions on sub-letting?
- What restrictions are there on selling the timeshare?
- What facilities can you use? Are they free?
- Do you have to retain the timeshare for a minimum number of years?
- What happens at the end of the timeshare period?

- What happens if you die? Can you bequeath the timeshare in your Will?
- Can you exchange your time period for a similar time period in another property?
- How is the management fee calculated?
- Are there any hidden extras?
- What are the rules for increasing the fee in the future?

Think of the future

It is important also to understand that timeshare is for a long time. However, although you may have bought the right to use the property, the property still belongs to the developer. He is running a business and businesses are bought and sold. You could find that at some time in the future, your developer sells out and you come under the control of a different management group. They may have different ideas as to what constitutes good management and, with the development profits all gone, they may be relying on the management fee to provide their future reward.

When buying your timeshare, therefore, do think carefully about what might happen in the future. Your safest option is to buy through reputable and financially secure companies but even that is no guarantee that the property that you have a timeshare in is going to stay with that developer. There's also no guarantee that that developer is going to stay independent because he may be bought out by another, larger developer.

The other reason for choosing a financially secure company (and it's easy enough to check on their financial stability) is to remember that you don't own the asset – they do. If they go bankrupt, you may lose the right to the asset completely and have no legal redress whatsoever.

Different forms of timeshare

Over recent years, a number of variations have grown up in the timeshare market.

Property by shares

This system effectively means buying shares in the timeshare company who may own a number of properties in a range of locations not necessarily all in Spain. Each share qualifies you for an annual allocation of points and you may 'spend' these points on weeks in any location or save them up for a future 'spend'. The more popular the location and the more popular the time period, the more points you need. The shares have a value and can be bought and sold, just like shares in a publicly quoted company.

Advance payment for hotels

A company set up for the purpose buys the right to use rooms in a range of hotels at certain times of the year for up to 20 years. These rights are sold to members of the company who buy the rights for a particular time period. They then have a choice of which hotel to spend their particular week or weeks in.

User rights in a holiday project

This is a similar system to the hotel system but where the company has purchased an entire complex. This is very similar to traditional timeshare because the users do not own the property but merely purchase the right to use a room in the property for a stated period of time.

The club concept

This is becoming increasingly popular. Instead of entering into an agreement to purchase a timeshare, you apply to take out membership of a club, one of the benefits of which is to provide you with the exclusive use of a designated apartment or villa for a stated time period. Once again, this gives you no rights to the property but it is a popular way for British companies to conduct their business because the relationship between you and the sales organisation is that between a club and its members (with the property being 'incidental'). Because of this, the whole organisation can be run according to UK law, not Spanish law.

In theory, the club system offers its members the right of say over the way the club is managed and members will be invited to an annual general meeting to discuss the way in which the club is run.

In some club systems, the period of time purchased is approximately 25 years though some are offering access to property in 'perpetuity'. It may also be stated in the club rules that after 25 years, the property will be sold and that the proceeds will be distributed amongst the 'owners'.

In most cases, the selling company will usually have set up an offshore trust who will hold the shares in the club for its members. However, because these trusts are set up offshore it is often difficult to obtain information on who the trustees are, the details on how the trust is managed, and on what action the trustees can take that would override the interests of members. Consequently, if you are considering purchasing membership of this kind of club, you should make quite sure that you see a copy of the club rules and also a copy of the trust deed in order that you fully understand exactly what you are entering into. You should also make quite sure that the company have complied with all the legal and fiscal obligations of any company resident outside Spain who own property in Spain.

Overall, a reputable club will have a well organised deed of trust and the company will be set up to run the club on behalf of club members in an ethical way.

Joint ownership

There is of course nothing wrong with clubbing together with family or friends to form a group of people who are interested in buying a property in Spain for their joint use. There are two ways in which this can be done:

1 You can, as a group of individuals, buy a property outright in Spain with all your individual names listed in the *escritura*. This would normally only be recommended for small groups of people (say no more than four) because the problems of sorting out the legal details with a larger group can be quite difficult.
2 A larger group of people could get together and form a company in the UK with the company then buying the property in Spain. This is a simpler route because the legal details are being handled by one entity (ie the company).

In many respects, this is no different from the growing practice of joint ownership in the UK. Faced with the rapidly increasing costs of properties, it is now quite common for two or more people to get together and pool resources in order that they can get a foot on the housing ladder. Once again, there are no legal problems involved in doing this but as with all joint ownerships it is most important that you agree amongst yourselves exactly what the rules are going to be in the future.

Consequently, if you are considering entering into this kind of arrangement with friends (or even your family) it would be very much in your interests to seriously consider drawing up a legal agreement between the members of the group so as to make it quite clear exactly what their rights and responsibilities are. Like most agreements, it will be designed to resolve problems before they arise – if you can't sort out your problems in advance, then perhaps you should think about buying your property with other people!

Amongst the sort of things this agreement should cover (and it can be easily drawn up through a solicitor in the UK) are the following:

- In what proportions are the individuals in the group going to pay for the property? There's no particular need for everybody to contribute an equal share but it should be clearly laid out that when the property is sold, each person receives back the equivalent proportion of the net proceeds.
- What proportion of the running costs is each person going to pay? This could well be done on an equal basis (on the grounds that it's difficult to divide up an electricity bill) but it could equally be done on the basis of usage over a 12 month period.
- What rights of access will each person have to the property? Will it just be by general agreement on a casual basis or will you allocate specific periods of the year to each person on a rota basis?
- When you're entering into this kind of agreement, you will expect it to run for a number of years. However, you should all agree on a certain date in the future when people can withdraw from the scheme and demand their share of the property, in cash. Your agreement should also cover what has to be done in those circumstances, for example:
  — Does the property have to be sold?
  — Can the other members buy out the share and, if so, on what basis is the price to be agreed?
  — Can other people buy into the group and if so, on what basis?
- Emergencies can, and do, arise. What action would be taken if one member is quite unable to continue with

the agreement because of financial problems? What happens if one of the group dies?

The list is not meant to be exhaustive and you may well have to draw up your own list. The only possible way of approaching this kind of agreement is to try and imagine every possible set of circumstances that could give rise to problems and make sure you have a solution for them.

Co-ownership is becoming increasingly popular and, given the right legal framework for it to operate, there's no reason why it shouldn't be an ideal way of buying property in Spain.

14 Living in a community

The law of horizontal property

In the majority of purchasing contracts which you sign when buying a property in Spain, you will find a clause which states that you accept the obligation to become a member of the Community of Owners and that you agree to the statutes. This is a particular feature of buying certain types of property in Spain – and it comes under a law which is known as the 'law of horizontal property'.

As you might expect, buyers of apartments could face some obligations applying to the entire building on the basis that they share the use of lifts, entrance halls and so on. But the law goes further than that – it can also apply where there are separate houses or where they are joined together in terraces or as part of the many village developments that have grown up in recent years in many of the Spanish coastal resorts.

By and large, where any proportion of the buildings are jointly owned or where there are common service areas such as swimming pools, gardens and private roads, all the owners in the community share the cost of maintaining the services and the laws of horizontal ownership may apply.

What the law requires

The law came into being in 1960 and has been virtually unchanged since then. It is now a requirement for any group of property owners who share common services to form a community and a developer or promoter who sells plots, houses or flats in such a development is obliged to make arrangements for the constitution of a community.

The way the law is put into effect is that the promoter draws up statutes by which he feels the community should be run. He determines the division between common elements and private property and decides in what proportion the common elements are to be allocated between each individual unit in the development. This information then becomes inscribed in the property register and the statutes also become part of the purchasing contract. Once the first sale has been made, the developer cannot change any part of these arrangements.

The fact that the law requires the promoter to do this work is no guarantee that he will do it or that it will be done fairly. There is nothing to stop the promoter from including restrictive statutes or from retaining part of the property for his own use. It is important therefore that you should study the statutes carefully before you sign the contract.

The law requires that every community should have its own statutes and as part of the contract, you will have to sign an agreement that you are prepared to abide by the statutes. These regulations define what part of the community property belongs solely to individual owners (which is normally everything behind your front door) and what parts of the community are jointly owned (which covers such things as the entrance hall to an apartment building, the lifts, all the wiring and piping of service installations and so on).

The law enables a community to be run in the way that the majority of owners wish and ensures that when problems arise, the community speaks as one voice. Consequently, though the administration may seem a little fiddly, it's important to get the workings of the community correct because there are significant advantages in doing so.

The obligations of owners

The basic obligations of all owners are laid down in law and they are designed to ensure that you look after your property where it affects other people and that you don't prevent other users from enjoying the use of their property:

- You must look after all the services to your property which are for the benefit of all the other owners as well (eg such as main water pipes, electrical wiring and so on).
- If any work has to be done on these common services, you must provide access for this work to be done.
- You must make good any damage that you cause to communal property.
- You must pay your proper share of the general expenses of the community (and if you don't, the community can demand payment and take you to court if necessary).
- You must follow all the rules of the community whether laid down by statute or passed by the general meeting.

Overall, the law merely expresses the general wish that everybody should be able to live in his home in peace and quiet. If at any time a member of the community consistently breaks this rule, the other owners can apply to the courts for the member to be deprived of the use of his property.

Your share of the community

It's important that you understand how much of the common property you own. Sometimes you will have an equal share of all the property that you jointly own; in other communities, the share will vary according to the size of the individual owner's house or flat. The share is called the *cuota* and it's important because it determines how much you will have to pay towards the cost of maintaining the common property and it also affects your voting rights at general meetings of the community.

In some cases, part of the development may not have been

specifically classified as common property and may have been excluded from the communal aspects by the developer.

The workings of the community

The community is run in a way which will be familiar to anyone involved in committee work in the UK. Most of the real work is done at the general meeting which is the governing body of the community. Such a meeting must be held at least once a year (the ordinary general meeting) though there could of course be other meetings called on an extraordinary basis.

The law sets down some rules on how a general meeting should be called:

- It must be done in writing and the notice must give the place, date and time of the meeting together with the agenda.
- The law states that the notice must be sent to your address **in Spain**. However, that does not rule out a copy of the notice being sent to your UK address **provided** this requirement is included in the statutes of the Community. If it isn't, then you should ensure that the matter is raised at the general meeting and the statutes amended.
- The notice must reach community members at least six days before the meeting (although this time limit is waived for extraordinary general meetings).

In many cases, of course, even six days aren't enough where owners live abroad. In these cases, there should be something in the statutes to say that notifications for general meetings should be sent to members with, say, 45 days notice. It may even be possible to fix a certain day for the Annual General Meeting, (for example, the first Saturday in each September) which then gives people plenty of time to make arrangements.

It's important that you attend all your community meetings or that you appoint somebody to attend them on your behalf. It is perfectly legal to arrange to be represented by proxy and it's important that you do. Unless the statutes prohibit it, the proxy need not necessarily be a member of a community and your proxy can also be in the form of a written signed document (but this is valid only for the one meeting). In the Appendix is an example of a letter appointing someone as your proxy.

You can also have a legal representative at a meeting. This could be in the case of minor owners or if you have given power of attorney to someone to represent your interests on your behalf.

The promoter himself may also take part in the community meetings on behalf of all unsold properties included in the community. In these cases, of course, he has full voting rights for all those properties – but he's also obliged to pay the corresponding part of the community fees as well.

Votes and voting

Everybody is entitled to vote at the meeting and their share of the vote is equal to their *cuota*. The law stipulates that there are two kinds of vote; situations where a unanimous vote is required and one where a simple majority is required.

The position where unanimity is required for a change in the rules are, for example:

— Changes in the *cuotas*.
— Changes in the statutes.
— Changes of communal elements to private elements.
— Major changes to the structure of the building.

For the decisions taken at the meeting to have legal weight, the decisions must be taken at a legally called meeting. This means a meeting where all the owners have been invited in correct time and where the agenda was distributed beforehand.

Also, the law recognises that it is impossible to insist that people either attend meetings in person or represent themselves in other ways. Consequently, based on a pure percentage of the total ownership of the property, it may be difficult to get any decisions taken even where only a simple majority is required. Under these circumstances, it is possible to follow the general meeting within a very short period of time (only half an hour for example), with a second meeting where a majority means simply a majority of the people **actually present** as represented by their *cuotas*. Under these circumstances, of course, the letter inviting members to the general meeting must make it clear that this procedure is going to be followed so as to give people every opportunity to have their views represented.

The minutes

An important aspect of all meetings of the community is that minutes have to be taken. It must have its pages numbered and they should be stamped by a local notary or judge. In the minutes, the following items must always be recorded:

- The people present at the meeting and whether or not they acted as representatives for other members.
- Who presided at the meeting and when and where it was held.
- The agenda that was sent out when calling the meeting.
- The discussions about the different points on the agenda, the main points of view expressed and the decisions taken and with what majority.
- The name of any member contesting the legality of any decision.

As with most committee meetings, the normal procedure is to read the minutes of the last meeting at the start of the next one and to have the minutes signed then.

Your right to object

It's also important that all absent owners are given information on what happened at the meeting and what decisions were taken. Absent owners have the right to register their disagreement with any of the decisions taken within one month of receiving the information. This means that any important decisions taken at a general meeting should not actually be executed until one month after owners who were not present at the meeting have received information about the meeting (unless they declare their agreement in the meantime).

In extreme cases, it is possible for any member of the community to appeal against the decision and to take the matter to a court of law if he thinks that a decision is against the law or the statutes. If, however, he wishes to complain on the basis that the decision is prejudicial to his interests, then he must be acting on behalf of members that represent at least 25% of the total *cuota* in the community.

One action you cannot take is to refuse to pay your fees because you disagree with what the community is doing. As a member of the community, you are required to pay the charges of the community at all times. If you don't pay, the community has a right to take you to court and, in a very extreme situation, to request the court to permit a public auction of your property.

The officers of the community

The president

The president is given a very important role to play by the law. He is the legal representative of the owners and is responsible for seeing that everything is conducted legally and in everybody's interests.

The president is elected in a general meeting by majority decision. He has to be a member of the community but needs no other special qualifications (ie he doesn't have to be Spanish). His term of office will last one year but would normally extend for a further year unless he asks to be relieved of his responsibilities or if he is asked to resign. In some communities, the statutes allow for the period of office to last for more than one year and this is perfectly legal.

Until a new president is elected, the old president must continue with the task. If the president leaves before a new president is elected or if he does not fulfil his obligations in any way, to the extent that it is harmful to the interests of the community, he can be taken to court by the community.

The responsibilities of the president are:

— To convene the general meetings.
— To preside over general meetings.
— To take action that has been approved by a general meeting.
— To represent the community in relation to matters affecting individual members.
— To represent the community in matters concerning people outside the community.

In order to discharge this responsibility he has quite wide powers of discretion granted him by the law. However, most of these powers have to be handed on to him by the general meeting ie the powers are not dictatorial!

Vice-president

There is no official position of vice-president in the law of horizontal property. That doesn't prevent the community from electing a vice-president but unless it's specifically mentioned in the statutes (or unless the statutes have been changed by unanimous decision at a general meeting), the vice-president has no formal legal powers and cannot deputise for the president.

The administrator

The administrator is given certain powers by law:

— He supervises the correct management of the total property.
— He prepares the annual budgetary proposals for the community.
— He undertakes the necessary collection of fees and, if any actions agreed at the general meeting involve payment, he will undertake to see that payment is made.
— He keeps the accounts of the community.
— He keeps the minute book and all other documents relating to the community's proceedings (unless a secretary has been elected to do this).

The administrator is elected by a majority at a general meeting and the duration is also for one year (unless otherwise allowed for in the statutes). Any community member can be elected as administrator but it's not necessary that the administrator is a member of the community. He will usually be paid for his work although in very small communities this would normally be waived. Payment would also be made to community members who act as administrator but the condition here is that they must have a work permit and must be taxpayers.

The secretary

The secretary is elected in the same way as the president and the administrator. The tasks of the secretary are:

— To send out the invitations to the general meeting as requested by the president.
— To take the minutes of the meetings.

— To send information to absent members on what was decided at the general meetings.

— To keep the minutes of the community and all other correspondence and documents.

— And to make these available to any member wanting to inspect them.

There is no reason why the president, the administrator and the secretary cannot be one and the same person. This will be quite usual in very small communities. In a community of fewer than four owners, an administrator need not be elected.

The language problem

In many communities, of course, the problem of language doesn't arise because most owners will speak a common language. However, that isn't always the case and it is the president's responsibility to arrange for interpreters to be present if he's aware that some of the members don't speak the common language. If there are owners from more than two or three language groups who can only speak their own language, the situation becomes difficult but it's up to the community to find the solution.

There is nothing in the law that says the community must hold the meetings in Spanish or even keep the records in Spanish. This means that the community can take the decision that it considers correct and convenient on the question of language. However, if a decision of the community is to be tested in a Spanish court then they will need records in Spanish or an authorised translation into Spanish of the relevant records.

From the promoter's point of view, he should always provide foreign language translations of the statutes according to the

nationality of the buyer in order that the buyer may fully
understand what the statutes contain.

Although community law appears fiddly that's the price of a
democratic system which ensures that your rights have been
looked after. It is important to make sure that you pay close
attention to your obligations under the community rules –
everybody is bound by the same rules and they ensure that
the community can run smoothly and effectively.

15 Extending your property

It seems to be a law of human nature that the first thing we do when moving into a new home (even one we have designed ourselves) is to think about how it can be improved. This may often be a quite conscious decision – we may have designed a basic house at the start with the full intention of extending it as time and money permit. The range of extensions of course can range from a simple carport to a substantial swimming pool with accompanying terracing but in Spanish law, an extension can mean even a very small development which appears trivial to those used to the relative freedom of action in the UK.

Small landscaping

By and large, you will have a fair amount of freedom as to what you can do in your own garden. If you live in the country on a *finca rustica* then you will have little or no restrictions on what you can do but you may have rather more if you have a plot within an urbanisation. Urbanisations often have limitations in the overall plans or in the community rules on what you can and cannot do. By and large, you'll always be able to plant trees and shrubs on your own property so long as they don't affect your neighbour's view or put his land in shadow. If you want to plant a hedge on the border to your neighbour's land you must have his agreement in writing – of course, he may change his mind later!

You also have the right to move the soil around as you wish and to level the ground where it seems appropriate. However, you should take care not to do anything that would cause a change in the natural flow of rainwater.

Walls and terraces

More extensive landscaping such as building walls or extending a terrace are more substantial and building permission is required. This is called a permit for *obra menor* (literally – smaller works) but of course it's not necessary to involve an architect. You can make a simple sketch of what you want to do, and present it to the Town Hall together with your application. At the same time you need to get an estimate of what it's likely to cost. The basic Town Hall fee for the licence is 2½% of the estimate And don't forget, there is now the new tax on building work to pay as well (see chapter 5).

You might be tempted to leave the matter of the licence in somebody else's hands ie the builder. Try to avoid doing this – if he forgets to make the application or fails to get the permit then you are responsible for the work that has been done. Responsibility means that the work can be stopped and you can be asked to put the property back to the state that it was in before you started.

On the back of the permit the Town Hall makes it clear that granting the permit doesn't prejudice the rights of third parties (ie if they give you permission to build a terrace that doesn't mean that you have the right to intrude on your neighbour's land). The permits are valid for six months and they can be transferred to another person if you sell the property.

More substantial work

If you undertake more substantial construction outside, such as a swimming pool or a garage (or even a large barbecue) then you need a building permit from the Town Hall. Under these circumstances, you have to give rather more detail of what you propose together with the plans and a simple building specification. The same form of permission is required to build a carport.

If the work is not too extensive, you won't need an architect and full plans. You just simply make a sketch of what you want to do together with a description of it, go to the Town Hall and get the permit for *obra menor*.

As far as the property itself is concerned, you are free to do anything that doesn't change the exterior of the building, or change the purpose of any of the rooms. What that means is that you can't put in an extra window in your basement or an additional door. It means that you can't tear down any load bearing walls inside the house that could put the building in danger of collapse and you can't change the classification of rooms (eg changing your garage into a guest flat).

However, if the changes are substantial (you want to knock down load bearing walls for example), then you'll need an architect to assist you and it may be necessary for you to obtain a full building licence.

Limitations

One point that you must bear in mind is that any plot has its building area and also its building volume. This can be just as important on a *finca rustica* as it is on an urbanisation.

Working out whether or not your extension will fall within the permitted guidelines can be tricky and it would be sensible to get competent help to do this. You may, for example, find that your extension is perfectly acceptable as far as the increased **volume** of the house is concerned, but that you can't have it all on the ground floor because the increase in **surface area** is too great (meaning that you can only achieve your objectives by having a two-storey extension).

In every case where the figures are in conflict (eg you are within the volume limits but over the surface area limits), then the lower limit prevails ie in this example you have to go for a smaller or higher extension.

For the owner of an apartment or any other type of community, it's important to know that you're not permitted to do anything that can alter the exterior design without first having the permission of the president of the community of owners. For larger changes a permit must also be had from the Town Hall. Inside your property, you are of course free to make any changes that don't affect any of the structural communal elements. But putting glass in your balcony or installing a parabolic TV satellite aerial, for example, can only be done with the agreement of the president.

Get an estimate

No matter how small the job appears to be, get an estimate (a *presupuesto*) before letting anybody start work. If you don't, they will be able to charge you anything they like and you will have to pay. So, always ask for a *presupuesto* and always get it in writing.

The tax and legal position

All extensions to existing property will carry *IVA* at the rate of 12% on the total bill (see chapter 10). That can be quite a large amount so you will have to bear that in mind when working out whether or not you can afford your extension.

The legal position is less straightforward. The basic problem is that you have written into your *escritura* the declared value of the property and it is this that will determine the capital gain on your property and also the amount of currency that you can export should you ever decide to sell your property. By spending more money on your property you are in theory increasing the property purchase price (ie reducing the capital gain) and also increasing the base on which the exportation of currency figure can be calculated. Unfortunately, the only way that this can be accommodated in practice is to amend the *escritura* and this can prove to be an extremely tedious process. If it is to be done at all, then it's done in the following stages:

- You will need a certificate from your bank showing that the money used for the extension has been paid for in convertible *pesetas* if you are not a resident.
- You will need evidence from the Director General of Foreign Transactions that they have agreed with the use to which the money has been put as evidence by the department sending you form TE7.
- You may then go to the notary and make up a notarised *escritura* for a declaration of new work (the *declaracion de obra nueva*).
- You can then go to the property registry and persuade them to add the inscription of the extension to the details on the property register.

Overall, the amount of time and effort that it is going to take up together with the fees that you might incur can make this a very expensive business. At the end of the day, it might be just as easy to pay the money for the extension and forego the capital gains and foreign currency exportation benefits. However, it is something to bear in mind when buying your house in the first place. If you firmly intend to extend the property in a fairly short period of time, then it might be better to arrange to borrow the money in the UK and pay the extra interest rather than suffer the additional capital gains tax and foreign currency problems at a future date.

16 Letting your property

There are two ways in which you can let property that you own in Spain:

1 You can let your property to people for an extended period of time, ie they regard it as their temporary home for several months.
2 You can let your property for short periods of time, ie for holidays.

Use as a temporary home

Under these circumstances, you will be allowing people to use your property for an extended period of time and so it is important that you make it clear from the start the basis on which the property is to be made available. The risk you run is that a loosely worded agreement could be interpreted as something other than temporary in which case your tenant obtains much more protection under the law. Most important from your point of view is that it could then become quite difficult to remove the tenant and for you to repossess your property.

Consequently, if you are considering the long-term letting of your property it is important to engage the services of a solicitor or an estate agent to get the agreement correctly drafted. The contract should contain a clause that expressly states that the letting is a temporary arrangement only.

It would be wise to ensure that your property is furnished (in which case you should prepare a full list of contents to be signed by your tenant). Letting an unfurnished house weakens your position in the event of a dispute as a judge may rule that an unfurnished dwelling cannot by definition be a temporary dwelling. To make quite sure that the position is clear, the contract should stipulate a total rent and then break this down into the proportion allocated to renting the property and the proportion allocated to renting the contents.

Obviously, you should choose your tenant with great care. The nuisance value of a bad tenant cannot be compensated for no matter how good the rent you are obtaining. Get as many references as you can from your prospective tenant, particularly a reference from his bank. If you are dealing with the letting yourself and not through an agent, then you will naturally wish to meet your tenant and make up your own mind about him.

Long-term letting of your Spanish property is no different from long-term letting of any other kind of property. There are dangers and it's up to you to take every possible precaution you can to make sure you're letting it to the right kind of people and that they fully understand that it is your property which at some point in the future you are going to want back.

Short-term letting

Many people buy property in Spain for their own holidays and then set out to cover some of their costs by letting out for holiday use when they don't need it. If you have a wide circle of friends and relations you may well be able to arrange this yourself but this has the disadvantage that you are dependent on people's good will to keep the property in good condition and to leave it clean and ready for the next occupant. Unless you can come to some arrangement with a neighbour in Spain to keep an eye on the property, you can anticipate some problems with people returning from holiday and complaining about broken lightbulbs, electrical equipment not working, etc.

The alternative is to hand the job over to a letting agent who will do everything for you, including routine domestic maintenance. The rents will be set by the agency and after deducting their costs they will pay the balance to you. The amount you can expect to receive will be written into an agreement but you are unlikely to get guarantees of income other than for a purely nominal amount.

The legal position

Any foreign property owner in Spain who lets his property for commercial purposes (except for use by members of his family or close friends), should report this commercial use of the property to the Spanish authorities and pay Spanish income tax on this income. If you have bought an apartment in a building classified as a tourist apartment (*apartamento turistico*) you need not make a report since this will have been done for the building or complex as a whole. If you decide to let through a tour operator, travel agent or letting agency, you should ask them if they have reported the letting to the authorities and make sure that they withhold (and pay in) the taxes on the letting income.

If you intend to let your family and/or friends use your property when you are not there, you should inform the provincial delegation of the Ministry for Tourism (you will find a suitable form of letter in the Appendix).

Letting through an agency

If you use your property for commercial letting, the agent handling it should apply for permission to use your property as an *apartamento turistico*. The permit is granted by the Minister for Tourism and his officials have the power to inspect your property to see if it is fit to be let. The agency is also required to deduct 20% of the net rental income (ie after they have deducted their expenses) which is then paid to the authorities as part of your income tax. When declaring the income in your tax return, you should declare the full net income and indicate clearly the amount the agency has deducted before paying the balance to you.

If you are buying property in a community (ie you are obliged to abide by the statutes of the community of owners), then make sure the statutes are not particularly restrictive in how the property may be used in your absence. Also, make sure there are no clauses in the purchase contract or in the title deeds which restrict your right to let other people use your property. In some cases, you may find that you have unrestricted rights provided you use the services of the building promoter's letting agency. It's not unusual to find these restrictions in the contract and, if you sign it, these restrictions become legally binding on you. Get your lawyer to check the position carefully before you sign the contract.

It's also important to choose your letting agency with great care. The majority are perfectly respectable and will treat you with honesty. Others are less than honest and will rely on the fact that you may probably be (literally) a thousand miles away and unable to check up on them.

By and large, you have to investigate the agencies which are offering their services and make your own judgment. The following guidelines may be helpful:

- Ask for references from satisfied users and go and see

them (or write to them) and ask for confirmation of their satisfaction. If the agency is unwilling to provide the names of satisfied clients, find another agency.

- Use well established companies and attempt to get some background information on their financial stability. Choose companies that have been operating for some time.
- Don't believe wildly optimistic figures of potential income. Get some brochures in the UK on the costs of renting holiday property in the area so you can get an idea of the likely weekly income that the agency will be receiving during the peak holiday periods.
- Don't believe promises that your property will be occupied all the time that you're not there. There is an over supply of available accommodation and although you may get 100% occupation during the peak holiday periods, you can expect lower than that during the off-peak season.
- Don't accept a percentage of the net rental income that is less than 60–75%. Make sure you receive payment as soon as the letting period has ended and don't be prepared to sit and wait for the agency to settle their account.
- Ask for confirmation that the agency have paid your tax deductions to the authorities.
- Check the position from time to time. Ask the agency for a regular schedule of lettings and then get a neighbour to check the property during periods when the property is apparently un-let.

With a good agent, you can expect a reasonable flow of income from your property. But don't be too ambitious – if you end up covering your running costs, you will have done well.

Combined accommodation

Another form of development is the *apartotel* which is essentially a block of apartments associated with a hotel complex or a complex having the facilities usually provided by a hotel (restaurant, swimming pool etc). The purchase of the apartment is handled in the usual way but the promoter will reserve the right in the contract to run the hotel aspect on a commercial basis (which could mean offering the use of the facilities to people other than apartment owners).

This, of course, could be a useful way of obtaining rental income. Because your apartment has these guaranteed facilities close at hand, it means that you will be able to offer a rather more complete 'package' to prospective tenants. However, you should not be too surprised if there is a condition in the contract that restricts letting to the developer through his own letting agency.

In some cases, the arrangements are even tighter. Although you own the property, the agreement from the start is that you have access to it for a certain number of weeks in the year only and during the rest of the time the promoter has the right to let it and pay you a percentage of the income. This is effectively a reversal of the timeshare principle; you have the same type of restricted access to the property but you do at least own the asset and can buy it and sell it in exactly the same way.

Other types of development based on this principle are villas (hence *villotel*) and pueblos (*pueblotel*).

The law before 1985

The present law on letting came into effect in May 1985 – the law before then was very beneficial to tenants and contracts issued before May 1985 are still governed by the old law. As in the UK, it is possible to buy property with a 'sitting tenant' so if you are faced with the choice of buying this kind of property (or if you inherit it) you should be aware of what the law provides for your tenant.

Under the old law, the tenant has three basic rights:

1 Limited increases in rent.
2 Automatic extensions of contract.
3 Strict limits to reasons for termination of contract.

By and large, the increases in rent that are allowable are very tightly controlled and are related to the cost of living. Any increases over and above this can be resisted (successfully) by the tenant.

The tenant has the right to extend the rental period and there can be very few reasons why this right can be withdrawn. Even if the tenant signs a document agreeing not to extend the contract, the document has no weight in law. If you can demonstrate that you have a desperate need for the property yourself then that may be a reason for terminating the contract, as will evidence that the tenant doesn't really need the property himself (possibly because he owns the property already). If you need the property yourself and can prove that fact, then you may still have to give the tenant up to twelve months' notice.

Even the death of a tenant does not necessarily mean the end of the contract. If his close relations have been living with him on an habitual basis, then they inherit the same rights as the tenant.

There are, of course, some rights to terminate the contract and these are usually related to failure to pay the rent (unless due to unemployment), sub-letting without permission, damaging the property or using it for an improper purpose. The tenant also has the right to terminate the contract if you fail to maintain the property and abide by the terms of the contract although the tenant also has the option of suing you for compensation.

Generally speaking, letting contracts entered into before May 1985 are bad news for the landlord and excellent news for the tenant.

17 Selling your property

Advance preparation

When buying a property in Spain you should always keep in mind the possibility that one day you might want to sell it again. You might find out that after some time you're just not cut out for life in Spain or that you can't use the property enough to justify its costs. On the other hand, you might be enjoying life in Spain so much that you now want to buy a different type of property having had a chance to look around for what really suits you.

The things to keep in mind at the time of purchase so that your property can be sold easily at a later date are:

- Make sure that you've tied up all the legal loose ends and that you have good title to your property.
- Make sure that your *escritura* has all the necessary bank certificates so that you don't have any problems in exporting the proceeds. Make sure that the sum written into your *escritura* is not too small – not only is it strictly illegal (although it is a time honoured custom) but it might cause you problems later on.
- Keep your property maintained and attractive looking. Some specialist organisations are now offering to keep properties in good decorative order for a fixed annual sum. If you're not able to maintain your home without help, this kind of service can help you and can also maintain the value of an expensive asset.

The legal position

Sales by residents

If you are resident in Spain (and for a full definition of this, see chapter 18), you can only sell your property in normal *pesetas* and you won't be able to exchange these *pesetas* for foreign currency. For this you have to give up your *residencia* (you can either let it expire or hand it in to the nearest police station). You are then a tourist again and you can prepare an application for repatriation of the proceeds from the sale of your property.

You are only allowed to export the money you imported in the first place (according to the bank certificate), plus a reasonable increase, which is decided by the Ministry of Commerce. The decision on repatriation of funds is normally routinely granted by the Director General of Foreign Transactions in Madrid, provided your papers are correct. This may take some time because the Ministry will wish to check whether you have paid all your taxes before leaving, especially any capital gains taxes resulting from the sale.

Under normal circumstances, any excess gain over and above the increased purchase price, will normally have to remain in Spain.

Sales by tourists

If you are a tourist, with a bank certificate of imported foreign currency in your title deed, you are free to sell your property to another non-resident foreigner and cash the money abroad. The new owner will also acquire your foreign currency rights attached to the original *escritura*.

Although you are able to evade Spain's exchange control laws by this route, you are still liable for the capital gains tax and it's possible that the new owner might have difficulties registering the property because of the unpaid taxes.

It is not necessary for such a sale to be made in Spain – it can also be made before a Spanish Consul General in Britain (because they are also notaries).

Things to watch

One important point is not to sign the title deed unless you have already received the purchase price in cash or it has been put into a blocked account where it can be released to you upon presenting a copy of the *escritura* in the name of the new owner. If your purchaser pays you with a cheque, the particulars of the cheque should be noted in the *escritura*.

The tax position

If you are resident for tax purposes in Spain (see chapter 11 for the definition), then your capital gains are included in your income **excluding** the capital gain that you make if you sell your main residence. If, however, you don't buy another Spanish property within two years of the sale, then you must declare the gain as part of your income.

That can be an important consideration if you are selling one property in Spain and buying another one. Make absolutely certain that the dates on the title deed follow one another ie that you clearly sell your first property before buying your second property otherwise you could find yourself with a tax liability on the capital gain made from selling your first house. The time of sale is the time of making the *escritura*.

You will find more details on the tax position in chapter 10.

Methods of selling

Private sales

One of the first decisions you must make when you come to sell your house is whether to use an agent or to undertake all the work yourself, which as an owner you are quite entitled to do. It is also possible to give power of attorney (a *poder*) to another private person to sell a property on your behalf. You do this before a notary, (which may be at a Spanish Consulate abroad if you wish), and the cost is normally quite small.

However, do take extreme care about the person to whom you give a power of attorney to sell your property. In some cases, some owners have never seen any of the money from the sale.

Sales through agents in Spain

If you ask an estate agent to sell your house, remember that only registered real estate agents (who can show you their registration number) are legally allowed to sell on your behalf. By law, they can charge any percentage on the sale that they are able to negotiate with you and they will usually ask you to sign a form which specifies this commission.

It's worthwhile taking care when signing this form because built into it (occasionally on the reverse side) may be a clause which gives them an exclusive right to sell on your behalf. If you decide to accept such a clause, you will be liable to pay the agent the agreed commission even if you sell your house without his help.

If you decide to give an agent an exclusive agreement (an *exclusiva*) then they are normally set for a fixed period during which you may not withdraw. You can of course negotiate the fixed period and normally three to six months should be enough time to entrust the sale to one agent.

The final point is to make sure that you agree the minimum price you are prepared to accept but also to make sure that the agreement states the commission to be paid **as a percentage** of the sale price. If you don't have that clearly defined, the agent could sell your property for much more than the agreed minimum sale price and, quite legally, pocket the difference.

Sales through overseas agents

It is perfectly legal for you to sell your property through an agent whose business is conducted outside Spain provided that the agent restricts himself to looking for buyers outside Spain. Once again, the commission charged is a subject of negotiation between you and the agent. In some cases, your agent may offer to accept payments in foreign currency from a potential buyer. There is nothing illegal in that but it's an area where you should take care. The very fact that the transaction is being conducted on an international scale between countries of different codes of conduct and different laws will make it harder for you to secure justice if your agent turns out to be less than honest or becomes insolvent.

18 Settling in

You have bought your property and now you are thinking of making it a more permanent arrangement, or perhaps of having a longer stay in Spain. What you have to decide now is whether or not you are a tourist or a resident. It's important at this point to draw the distinction between being **legally** resident and resident for **tax purposes**. Chapter 11 explains the tax position and this is determined by rules outside your control. Your legal status in Spain (ie whether you are a tourist or a resident) is to some extent a matter of choice but you cannot just become a resident – there are forms to fill in.

What you must understand, however, is that the two types of residence are different – you can technically be a tourist in Spain but still be regarded as resident for tax purposes.

Tourist or resident?

The question of whether to stay in Spain as a tourist or to become a resident is a little vague in some areas. Basically, as a UK citizen, if you visit Spain as a tourist you're allowed to remain there for 90 days without requiring a visa provided, of course, you have a valid passport to present to the authorities when you arrive in Spain.

Tourist status has some advantages for people staying in Spain for short periods. They are allowed to open certain types of bank accounts that residents can't open and also to drive a car on foreign plates for a limited period of time.

There's a quirk in Spanish law which allows you to prolong your stay in Spain without applying for official permission. This is to leave the country briefly – even for one day – at the end of your authorised period to get a new entry stamp on your passport. However, a better route for anybody who wishes to remain in Spain for more than the ordinary 90 day permit is to apply for a *permanencia*.

The *permanencia*

The *permanencia* is a document which will allow you to stay in Spain for a further 90 days as a tourist. To obtain one you will need the following papers:

- A passport containing a current entry stamp (ie you don't need a visa).
- Three passport sized photographs.
- A statement from your Spanish bank showing that you have at least 250,000 *pesetas* in your account or that you receive regular pension payments.
- The names of your parents.

Armed with this documentation, you can go to the nearest main police station (*comisaria de policia*) with a foreigners' department and they will provide you with the necessary document.

Once you have had one *permanencia* you must either leave Spain or have started the process to obtain your *residencia*. One point you must be alert to is that if you spend more than 182 days in a calendar year in Spain you will be regarded as resident for tax purposes (see chapter 11).

The *residencia*

The *residencia* is the permit which is normally valid for two years when it is first issued. To obtain one, you will need the following papers:

- Your current passport stamped with a current visa from a Spanish Consul in the UK (note – this visa **cannot** be obtained in Spain).
- Four passport photos in colour.
- A certificate from the local British Consul in Spain that you are resident in Spain (one certificate is sufficient for a married couple).
- A certificate that you have no criminal record in your home country.
- A *Papel de Estado* which is a form of payment to the State which you obtain from an *estanco* (tobacconist).
- A certificate from your Spanish bank giving your current bank balance or your regular monthly pension income or other income.
- Evidence that you belong to a private health insurance scheme valid in Spain and/or have rights to the Spanish National Health Insurance (in some places you may be asked for both).
- Evidence of accommodation (which could either be your *escritura*, a long-term rental contract or receipts for rent paid).
- The first names of your parents.

How to obtain your *residencia*

Residencias are obtained from the foreigners' department of the police station which serves your area but it is often useful to let a *gestor* do the work for you. If you use a *gestor* to make your application, you should go to him at least 45 days before your visa expires. When your application for *residencia* is accepted, you will be issued with a *resguardo*, a special receipt which, together with your passport, forms sufficient identification for you in Spain until your *residencia* is ready for you to collect. The *resguardo* also enables you to travel in and out of Spain if necessary without requiring a current visa. It is normally valid for two months but may be renewed where it was obtained if your *residencia* is not ready for collection.

Renewing your *residencia*

The *res·dencia* is normally valid for two years for the first time, but renewals are for five years. The renewal procedure is basically the same procedure as before and it is recommended that application for renewal should be made at least one month before the *residencia* runs out. You will need the same documents as before but, in addition, you will require evidence that you have made an income tax return for Spain (even if it is negative) and whether or not you pay taxes in the UK. You will also require a certificate of good conduct from the Spanish Ministry of Justice. You can get this by going to the nearest *estanco* asking for a *Certificado de Antecedentes Penales*, completing it and sending it off to Madrid.

The document regarding your financial situation is usually a certificate of the state of your account issued by your Spanish bank. If you are receiving a regular income from the UK, then a certificate of the amount being paid to you will also help as well. There are no strict rules concerning exactly what is required and the criteria vary from area to area. The police will tend to have doubts about people whose income does not reach 50,000 *pesetas* a month as the main purpose of this check is to prevent potential illegal workers from remaining in Spain.

Apart from that, the only possible reason for a resident's permit being denied is evidence of anti-social behaviour on your part during the first period of your stay!

The benefits of *residencia*

Residencia normalises your situation if you're living permanently in Spain. It offers you greater protection and grants you rights enjoyed by Spaniards in case of problems or serious accidents. In addition:

- You may buy a Spanish car or get a loan from a bank to buy a car (or a house).
- It allows you to apply for a work permit in Spain. If you are granted a work permit, you will receive a five year resident's permit and your family will also be entitled to this level of protection.
- You obtain the right to open a savings account and gain the right to export more foreign currency without permission (although, a disadvantage is that you have to close certain accounts which you may have opened as a tourist).

Becoming a tourist again

If at any time you wish to become a tourist again, then you can either let your *residencia* expire or you can ask for it to be cancelled by handing it in to any police station which has a foreign department.

Making the move

Once you've bought your property in Spain, then you're going to have to furnish it. You will of course find that Spain has all the furniture that you will ever need on offer at a wide variety of prices. Nevertheless, many people do like to bring their memories from home with them and, in some cases, your second-hand furniture will be much cheaper than buying new furniture in Spain.

Taking up temporary residence

When you buy a property in Spain to use as a tourist you may import furniture and personal goods into Spain **free of import duty**. However, you will only receive exemption from *IVA* (the Spanish version of VAT) if these goods come from a country in the Common Market. To obtain the exemption from *IVA*, you must also provide the following documents:

- An application for exemption with both your address abroad and the address of your second home in Spain.
- Proof that you are the owner of the property in Spain or have rented it for a long period.
- A list of the items to be imported, stamped by the Spanish Consulate at the point from which you exported them.
- A signed statement that you undertake not to let your second home to others.

One of the rules that you must follow, however, is that all the goods you import must have been in your possession and in use for at least six months before you bring them into the country. In order to avoid any doubts which might arise at the customs, it would be helpful to bring with you evidence of the date of purchase. But do bear in mind that the rule is six months **of use**. If you bring in material which is quite obviously brand-new and has never been used, then you can expect some problems and you may find yourself having to pay tax on it.

It would be helpful to prepare a duplicate list of all the items you intend bringing into Spain (in Spanish) and write down the value of each item. You set the value and, considering that the goods are used, you may tend to make it rather low. But don't make it **too** low, otherwise you may have problems with this value with the customs.

The procedures and payment

You will be asked to pay a deposit (or put up a guarantee) to cover both the *IVA* and the import duties. Provided that you can prove that you are still the owner of the items in question, the deposit on the *IVA* will be returned to you in 12 months and that on the import duties returned within 24 months. Sometimes, you will be required to provide proof of ownership – this is done by asking a notary to make a statement that they are still in your Spanish home.

The amount of the deposit or guarantee that you will be required to make in taking goods to Spain is determined by the relevant customs at the point of entry. Variations are not uncommon – in some cases, 60% of the declared value of the goods is required as a deposit.

Taking up permanent residence

By law, you are allowed a 12 month period from the date of leaving the UK during which you may import to Spain not only furniture and personal goods but also luxury items like your car, motorcycle, caravan, boat and private aircraft. However, some customs officials are rather more eager than the law allows and prefer to adopt a 6 month time limit. It might be better to opt for safety and work to the shorter time scale.

Used furniture and personal items (but not luxury items) may be imported free of import duty and *IVA* subject to the following conditions:

- You must supply the customs with a detailed list of the goods to be imported, with an indication of their approximate value, stamped by the Spanish Consulate at the point of export.
- You must submit an application for exemption, and the application must carry your home address in Spain or your provisional address if you've not yet built or bought your home.
- At the place where you import your goods, you must provide:
  (a) a certificate of your application for exemption.

   (b)   your new *residencia*. If you are unable to present your new *residencia* at the time of importation, a deposit of 60% of the declared value of the goods or guarantee will be demanded. This will only be refunded if the *residencia* is presented **within the 12 month time limit** (although as explained earlier it would be safer to assume that a 6 month limit applied).

   (c)   a certificate from the police who issued the *residencia* to say that it is your first one.

   (d)   a *certificado de baja de residencia*. This is a certificate (eg a letter) drawn up in the UK, issued by an official source which gives the date on which you left your residence in the UK. You may find it a little difficult to draw up a *certificado de baja de residencia* because, in practice, the only authorities which the Spanish customs accept are the police. However, a way round the problem is to make a declaration, before a Spanish Consul in the United Kingdom, or the British Consul in Spain, that you intend to leave the United Kingdom and start living in Spain.

- If you wish to import your car or motorcycle, you must present proof that the vehicle has been registered in your name for at least six months before you left the UK. You must also prove that VAT has been paid on the vehicle and not returned to you. As explained earlier, if the VAT paid is lower than *IVA* in Spain, you will have to pay the difference.

- The exemption is given on goods imported within a period of 6 months after you have established your permanent residence in Spain, or after having cancelled your residence in the UK. The goods can be imported once or several times, within these time limits.

Once goods have been imported into Spain, they cannot be sold to another person for at least 12 months.

Rules for luxury items

Cars, motorcycles, caravans, boats and private aircraft can all be imported into Spain but they will be subject to *IVA*. The *IVA* to be paid is the difference between the Spanish rate of *IVA* on the day of importation and any similar tax (eg VAT) which has been paid and not refunded in the country from which they originated.

If you are required to pay any *IVA* in this way, then it will be levied on the customs valuation of the item concerned. You should be aware that such a valuation may be higher than the value you place upon the item.

The other thing to be aware of with these luxury items is that although you may be able to import them, that in itself does not give you the right to use them. After they have been imported, they will be subject to stringent tests by the Ministry of Transport before licences are granted.

The marine requirements, for example, are likely to be significantly more demanding than you are used to in the UK.

Using a removal firm

In view of all the problems of importation, it could be very worth your while relying on a removal company of international experience as they will be familiar with the practices at many customs points. Alternatively, if you decide not to use a removal firm, you may find that you will need the services of an *agente de aduanas*, (a customs agent), at the point of entry. However, you should realise that the customs **agent** is not a customs **official** and so you should obtain from the agent a full set of receipts for any money you pay him showing what duties he has paid on your behalf and what his charges are for making the arrangements.

Insurance

Another point you should consider is the insurance of your goods in transit. If you are using a removal firm, you will probably find on reading the small print of the contract, that the remover will absolve himself of all responsibility for damage or loss and rely on the insurers to pick up the bill.

You may be tempted to declare low values for your goods for the sake of paying a smaller deposit on the *IVA* and import duties – but, by the same token, you cannot insure the goods for higher values than you have declared. It therefore makes sense to be realistic in your valuation and not to declare a low value which could lead to problems if the goods are damaged in transit.

Cars

The tourist

As a tourist, you can drive your own car freely in Spain on your own UK driving licence (although it still makes sense to get an international driving licence as Spain hasn't completely caught up with Common Market regulations). It's not necessary to have a 'green card' although it might make sense to do so because, without it, your insurance policy may only give you the minimum legal cover required in Spain and this may not be enough. Also, if you are driving your car to Spain, you must of course consider the requirements for licences and insurance in the countries that you travel through on the way. It is also important that you have a valid MOT certificate, valid UK road tax and that your driving licence is in order. Your insurance cover could be invalidated if these requirements are not met.

If you want to stay in Spain as a tourist longer than the six months normally allowed, then you can apply for an 'extension of temporary importation' for your car. This application must be made before the tourist period for the car runs out and before you are granted a *residencia*.

The extension (which will last for six months) will be granted on payment of duty equal approximately to 10% of the import duty. This exercise may be repeated four more times which gives you a total of approximately five years legal driving in Spain on foreign plates. (You should of course be fully aware that a car on foreign plates which is illegally in Spain may be confiscated and that there will be a heavy fine to pay in addition to the duty.)

If you are unable to get an extension, you must either take the car out of Spain or have it sealed (see below).

Leaving your car in Spain

If you come to Spain for several short vacations a year which total less than the six months per calendar year, then you can leave your car permanently in Spain. However, when you are away from Spain, you have to get the customs' authorities to seal your car. This is done by getting a special form from the local station of the *guardia civil*. They will arrange for your garage to be sealed (or, alternatively, that the registration plates are taken off and held by them). When you return to Spain, the process must be reversed. If you are away from Spain for a period of two months or longer, then your car should be sealed in any case.

Driving on tourist plates

You can buy a new car in Spain and register it with Spanish tourist plates. The purchase has to be through a special sales agent who may also sell second-hand cars that were previously registered with tourist plates. When applying for this, you must be able to declare that you haven't been in Spain for more than six months in the same calendar year and that you or your spouse are not engaged in business or work in Spain. You don't have to pay any import duty or luxury taxes on such a car but you do have to pay for it in foreign currency (or convertible *pesetas*).

The saving in relation to buying a normal Spanish registered car is approximately 35%. The tourist plates are normally valid for twelve months but you can obtain an extension provided you are still eligible. Always apply in good time before the expiration – the authorities take a very dim view of somebody driving with tourist plates without permission.

Spanish tourist plates offer some advantages but their greatest drawback is that no-one other than you (ie the owner) is permitted to drive. This could be slightly problematical – if your car breaks down for example, a garage mechanic will not be able to drive it for you.

Buying a Spanish registered car

As a tourist, you may find it difficult to buy a Spanish registered car (other than with tourist plates). In some areas they will sell you one and only ask for your passport. In other areas, they will sell you one if you have a document from the local authority certifying that you own property there and live there regularly. Other areas will only permit you to buy a Spanish registered car if you have a *residencia*.

But beware. If you are successful in buying a Spanish registered car, you might find it difficult to sell it in the future because people will say that they're not allowed to buy cars from a tourist (including, occasionally, the salesman who sold it to you in the first place!)

The resident

As a resident, you can only buy a car with normal Spanish plates and you cannot drive a foreign registered car unless you've got an extension as mentioned before. Remember also that the application for permanent importation of your car must be presented within six months of obtaining your first *residencia*. It can be a lengthy process, so a good tip is to apply for importation when you apply for your *residencia*.

Importing your second-hand car

If you are to import your car free of duty you will still have to pay the difference between VAT in the UK and *IVA* in Spain on the date of importation. Once you are through the importation procedure, you should not drive your car until the Ministry of Transport has issued temporary registration plates (green ones). These are valid for a short time but will enable you to drive to the nearest testing station for a rigorous test which your car must pass before it will be given a Spanish registration number. This is called the *matriculacion* and once you have this, you may then buy permanent white number plates. Altogether, importing a car is a difficult and time-consuming business and if you only need a small runabout, it's probably better to buy a car in Spain.

Driving licences

If you normally live in Spain or have lived there for more than one year, you must hold a Spanish driving licence. All residents of Spain who apply for a driving licence now will be issued with a new pink European driving licence. If you are about to take up residence in Spain and already hold such a licence, you may have to change it. In some parts of Spain the authorities will still expect you to have a Spanish licence.

The easiest way to get your new licence is to use the services of a *gestor* or the Royal Automobile Club of Spain. As a member of the European community, you may use your Spanish driving licence to drive Spanish registered vehicles in other EEC countries and also to drive vehicles registered in other EEC countries in the country of registration. In other words, you may use your Spanish driving licence to drive a British registered car while in Britain but you may not use your Spanish driving licence to drive a British registered car in Germany. As though you ever wanted to!

Tax and insurance

On an ordinary Spanish registered car you must pay (to your local authority) a small annual sum which depends on the horse-power of the car. On the question of insurance, as the owner of a car with Spanish plates, you are required by law to take out third party insurance cover. You can also take out fully comprehensive insurance and also cover for personal injuries. The level of cover (and the premiums) have been rising steadily in recent years to make them comparable with those in other EEC countries.

Some insurance companies in Spain offer a no claims discount of up to 50% for drivers who have not had an accident in several years but the cost of comprehensive insurance is relatively high in Spain. Many people, therefore, take out a cheaper cover for legal costs – in order to be able to recover their costs from the other party.

Business and work

As a member of the EEC, if you want to work as a self-employed person in Spain, you should now have the same right to do so on the same terms as a Spanish person. However, nothing is always straightforward and you might find yourself coming up against officialdom and your application being rejected for all manner of strange reasons. In broad terms, the procedure that you have to follow is no different from that required of a Spaniard and it is as follows:

- You will need, first of all, to go to the Inland Revenue authorities (the *Hacienda*) and take out what is called a 'fiscal licence' to undertake the particular work you have chosen (there are some 1,000 such activities, each with its own fiscal code number).
- Fiscal licences cost different annual sums for different activities. The licence carries your fiscal number, an

obligation to make a quarterly declaration of payment of *IVA* and to present annual accounts and an income tax declaration.

- You may be required to provide proof that you have the right to use the premises where you intend setting up the business and you may also have to provide evidence that your proposed business is viable.

- You then go the nearest police station with a foreigners' department and get hold of the all important purple card issued by the Minister of the Interior known as your *Tarjeta de Residente Comunitario* (the community card) which will contain your finger prints and a photograph. You must also arrange to make obligatory self-employed contributions to *Seguridad Social* which will cost you approximately 14,000 *pesetas* a month and which gives you access to Spain's National Health Service. It also gives you the opportunity, when you come to official retirement age, to lump your contributions in Spain together with your contributions in other EEC countries to provide a single state retirement pension paid from the country of your choice.

If you intend taking up one of the professions, then there may be professional codes and limitations that you will be subjected to. For example, a doctor must, before he can practice, have his qualifications accepted by the Medical College of the province and by any other specialist bodies that control his discipline. He must also (and quite rightly) be able to show that he is in good standing with the Medical Authorities or Associations in the UK.

Other professions may find that the door is not yet wide enough for this validation of their qualifications to take place. It's not particularly usual for a lawyer to be accepted for resident practice without Spanish qualifications. At a more mundane level, there is no sign of the College of Real Estate Agents admitting foreigners either.

Obtaining employment

If you wish to be employed in Spain, you must, before you leave the UK, obtain a suitable visa from your nearest Spanish consul. You must also have a contract of employment with a *bona fide* employer in Spain who will pay your social security contributions by deducting them, together with income tax, from your earnings. However, having a visa and a contract of employment is not the end of the story because you will not be permitted to work until a work permit has been secured for you.

Obtaining a work permit

Getting hold of a work permit may take several months, if it can be achieved at all. Both employers and prospective employees have to understand that there is an established 'pecking order' for the available jobs. The local delegation of the Minister of Work, who share with the police the responsibility for issuing work permits, ensure (naturally enough) that the first opportunity to fill available vacancies goes to Spanish citizens.

Next in line are Gibraltarians and nationals of other countries with special cultural links with Spain – and this would include EEC citizens as well.

The rules of issuing work permits are complicated; they vary from province to province and change frequently. At the end of the day, the granting of a work permit is at the discretion of local officials according to their view of the labour market in their own areas. In some areas, you will not get a work permit unless the work requires special skills or experience which local Spanish people do not possess.

As soon as you are working legally, your dependants may enter Spain with simply a passport and they will be granted a community residence card on request.

Once you have held a work permit for 12 months, your position is much more secure. You will then be entitled to a five year renewal period and the renewed permit will no longer be restricted by territory, activity, industrial sector or employer. Moreover, your spouse and children under 21 will also acquire certain rights to unrestricted work and residence.

If you have worked in Spain before then you might be interested to know that you also have certain residence rights on reaching the age of 65 or if your work ceases for reasons beyond your control. You have a two year period in which to lodge an application and if this is successful, you may well be granted a five year community residence card.

Starting your own business

As with any kind of enterprise, you should take all the necessary precautions you can and do some thorough homework before thinking about working in Spain. The streets are **not** paved with gold in the tourist areas of Spain and a number of businesses have failed dismally after starting with high hopes. As a guideline, it is wise to have enough capital at your disposal to live through the first year without making any profit at all.

One of the most frequent disaster areas is opening a bar in Spain. People often come on holiday to Spain, like the 'ambience' and decide that the ideal life for them is to open a bar or restaurant. If this is you, think again. Be especially wary if someone tries to sell you the *traspaso* (a sort of lease) of a bar, as if you can just walk in and start up a business, because you can't. You will need a fresh licence to open a bar and the Town Hall frequently set higher standards than they did to the people who preceded you. Don't buy a bar or restaurant or make any other important decisions about the business until you are sure that you will have the necessary permits from the Spanish authorities. In any event, bear in mind that the number of bars in Spain in the tourist areas is enormous, in order to service the very high summer tourist population. In winter (and you are going to have to live through winter as well), the resident population tends to drop quite dramatically.

The taxes you must pay

Almost all self-employed people must charge *IVA* for their work, normally at 12%, and this must be declared and paid quarterly in addition to your income tax payments. Unlike the UK, there is no threshold of earnings below which you are exempt from this obligation. You will probably need a tax expert to help you with this (known as an *asesor fiscal*).

Employing other people

On the assumption that your business is successful, you may decide to start employing other people and you should make yourself familiar with Spain's employment laws before doing so. Compared to the UK, they are extremely generous to the employee but not so generous to the employer.

Overall, if your business has grown to the point where extra help is required, it might be worth engaging the services of an *asesor laboral*, a specialist in all problems relating to employment and self-employment.

Really settling down in Spain

Because of the number of foreigners living in Spain, it's inevitable that some of them may wish to get married there, be it the case of two foreigners or that of a foreigner and a Spaniard. It is also quite common to find a foreigner who has settled in Spain and wants to give up his nationality and become a Spanish citizen.

Marriage

Two foreigners can enter into a civil marriage in Spain. This can be done at either of their embassies or before a Spanish judge in the local civil registry.

Getting married in Spain does, however, require a fair amount of paper work and so some people find it convenient to get married in Gibraltar, both from the point of view of rapid marriage and also from the point of view of rapid divorce! For two foreigners to be married in Gibraltar, they don't need to reside there – all they need is an affidavit giving all the personal information that is required.

Spanish nationality

Spanish nationality can be obtained after a ten year residence in Spain. You have to make a personal application to the Minister of Justice who is entitled to refuse it on the grounds of public order or national interest.

The period of ten years is reduced to one year for all those born on Spanish territory, or born outside Spain to a Spanish father or mother or for those who have married a Spanish citizen (even if the marriage has been dissolved).

Arranging your investments

Once you have settled down in Spain, then you need to be reassured that you are going to have a ready source of income especially if you are dependent on income from the UK, such as a pension. Under those circumstances, you will then have no difficulty at all in arranging any personal or company pension to be paid direct to your bank account in Spain (although some employers will probably prefer to pay it to a UK bank account and for you then to arrange a transfer to Spain yourself).

If you go to live in Spain before you have reached state retirement age (which is 65 for a man or 60 in the case of a woman), it would be sensible to arrange to continue to pay contributions in order to qualify for an old-age pension. When you are working in the UK you will normally pay class I contributions (class II if self-employed). When you are in Spain, it will be sensible to continue to pay class III (non-employed contributions) in order to ensure that you qualify for your full pension.

Your local office of the DSS will be able to supply you with the necessary information. You should then make an application to the DSS overseas group in Newcastle-Upon-Tyne, who will then make arrangements for you to continue paying your class III contributions, (and the simplest method is by a single yearly instalment paid to a British bank).

Provided that you have been credited with the required number of contributions throughout your working life, you will receive your old-age pension at state retirement age. British pensioners in Spain receive exactly the same pension they would have if they were living in Britain and they are entitled to the annual increase based on increases in the British cost of living.

You and the Town Hall

Spain is divided into 16 autonomous regions which in turn are made up of groups of provinces. Each province is divided up into municipalities and these are similar to the local authorities in the UK. They have autonomy in the administration of their own interests and they are financed not only by local taxes but also by a contribution from central

Government which depends on the number of people registered in the *Padron Municipal* (which is broadly the same as the Register of Electors).

Council members are elected in the Municipal Elections which are held every four years, the next ones being in 1991. A new law now gives foreigners residing in Spain the right to vote in these elections if their country of origin grants the same right to Spanish citizens.

The Council elects a Mayor (the *Alcalde*) and one or more Deputy Mayors. They also elect those council members who have responsibility for special areas such as urban matters, tourism and so on.

If you are buying property in Spain, then it's useful to get to know the Town Hall in your locality. You might need their assistance from time to time and it's useful to know where to go and how to get the answers to your questions. It's also important to get to know about the annual taxes and charges that the Town Hall will expect you to pay.

Each Town Hall has an information board where they publish announcements that concern local inhabitants. It's well worthwhile keeping up-to-date with this information because it could also tell you about new roads, electricity lines and other planning decisions that can affect your property.

As a taxpayer, you have a right to visit the Town Hall and ask for help. You shouldn't feel embarrassed about doing this – most Town Halls are happy about the presence of foreign property owners and want to give them the same service as they would give to Spaniards. In many of the tourist municipalities they have English speaking employees which could be helpful in sorting out any knotty problems.

In 1984, a new law also gave residents the right to vote in municipal elections. This is granted on the 'principle of reciprocity' meaning that the right is extended only to those countries who give the same rights to Spanish citizens in the same position). Unfortunately, this means that people from the UK are denied a vote in local elections and this is being pursued by the Euro MP, Mr McMillan Scott, who is trying to get the UK Government to relax its restrictions. It is hoped that the position does improve – being asked to contribute a growing proportion of the local rates without having any say in how those rates are spent is not particularly satisfactory. However, the situation is improving – proposals have recently been submitted in the European Parliament that would effectively grant a vote to citizens of the European Community residing in another community country.

How to participate

Decisions taken in the Town Hall are going to affect you. There will be decisions on taxes, how the taxes are going to be spent, decisions on roads, decisions on building plans and on a whole range of similar matters. Normally, there are no communication problems at all but it is useful for you to be able to put your point of view knowing that it has the full support of the law.

Consequently, the best thing you can do is to get yourself in a position where you can make your voice heard and that means registering yourself on the *Padron Municipal*. This is a list of all the people who live in the municipality and who aren't registered in any other municipality in Spain. You can register yourself if you haven't any property yourself but are staying in Spain on a long-term rental basis.

Once again, there is no disadvantage in being registered and the Town Hall certainly aren't going to prevent you. As the amount of financial support which they get from the State is dependent on the number of people registered on the *Padron Municipal*, the Town Hall are more than happy for you to include your name.

19 Health and health insurance

For the holiday maker, health insurance is no problem. There are a number of British insurance companies who offer inexpensive holiday cover and your travel agent will always be pleased to give you details. It's a small expense which you shouldn't neglect to indulge yourself in. Good health, or an accident free life, can never be guaranteed – and holidays are no exception. It also pays you to insure your luggage because it is not entirely unknown for your holiday belongings to disappear between your home and your holiday home.

For the resident, the position is not quite so straightforward. Unless you are a pensioner, you won't have access to the Spanish health service and so it is most important that you take out (or continue) private medical arrangements. Indeed, if you are hoping to take up residence in Spain and you are not a pensioner, you will not be able to get your *residencia* without evidence of contributions being paid to private medical insurance.

Reciprocal medical care

Reciprocal medical care is available to you in the EEC if you're a short-stay visitor eg if you're on holiday, or abroad on family visits. Treatment is usually limited to urgent cases of illness or accident and it is provided free or at a reduced cost depending on the health care schemes operating in each country.

Full details of treatments available can be found in DHSS Leaflet SA30 1986 which you should read carefully. This also includes an application form E111 and this form must be taken with you if you are travelling to Spain. To be eligible for E111 you merely have to be a British citizen and currently living in the UK. The form is obtained by filling in form CM1 (found in the centre of leaflet SA30 1986) and sending it to your local Social Security Office some weeks before your visit. When it is issued, it is valid for up to two years. When you arrive in Spain you should send your form to the provincial directorate of the *Instituto Nacional de la Seguridad Social (INSS)* (you will find the address in the local telephone book). They will then send you a book of vouchers and a list of available doctors and they will also give you information about the services that you can obtain under the scheme and the charges that are made.

Dependants (wife and children under 16 or under 19 if in full-time education) are also eligible regardless of their nationality and whether or not they travel abroad alone.

Under the reciprocal arrangements, you will be entitled to treatment but only for conditions needing **immediate** attention during the visit. Arrangements for free or reduced cost treatment only apply if similar treatment will be provided by doctors or hospitals in the UK. Not all costs are refundable but the local INSS office in Spain will pay those that are. If you have to have treatment which incurs a cost, make sure that you apply for a refund before you return to the UK because you might find it very difficult to recover the expenses once you've left Spain. You can expect to get hospital treatment and other medical treatment free; you may have to pay some fees for prescribed medicines and dental treatment.

The medical services

Doctors and dentists

There are very few places that are not within easy reach of qualified doctors. If you are buying property in the more popular resorts on the Spanish coast, you will normally be able to find English speaking doctors close by. Access to them is much the same as in the UK – they will have their surgery times but, in case of serious illness, they will also make house calls.

Once the doctor has prescribed the necessary medical treatment, all prescriptions (including injections) are obtainable from a chemist (a *farmacia*). For the injection itself, it is then necessary to go to the office of a qualified nurse known as a *inyeccionista* who carries out the injection.

In many of the coastal towns you will also find emergency first aid posts (*Clinica de Urgencia*) which have a wide range of surprisingly sophisticated treatment including such things as x-rays and electro-cardiograph scans. These are usually clearly signposted and can deal with a range of emergencies – but at a fee which can be quite expensive.

Dental treatment is also well catered for in most Spanish towns. Once again, like doctors, you will find that there are English speaking dentists in the more popular coastal areas.

Chemists

Farmacias are to be found in every town and village. As in Britain, they often operate a late night service so that there is usually always a chemist open somewhere not too far away.

You will find that they stock a range of patent medicines as well as items which are only available on prescription.

Because most of the main medicines are supplied by the international drug companies, you will find that most of the medicines that you are familiar with in Britain are to be found in Spain as well.

Medical insurance for residents

Pensioners

Under the European Community social security regulations, pensioners are entitled to health care from doctors and hospitals through the Spanish social insurance scheme under the same terms as those which apply to Spanish pensioners. If you are currently living in Britain and want to find out more about the Spanish scheme, you should write to the *INSS* in Madrid.

These new rules came into force on 1 January 1986 so if you are a resident in Spain who has been subject to a pension deduction under the previous agreement between Britain and Spain, then you should ensure that this deduction is no longer being made. If the DSS has not already written to you on form OVB–510 then you should contact the DSS overseas branch in Newcastle-Upon-Tyne.

In certain cases, British pensioners have considered it advantageous to exchange all their social security rights in the UK (both health and pension) for equivalent rights in Spain. That decision may well depend on your age and also your record of national insurance contributions while you were living in the UK but it could be worth your while getting information from both the DSS overseas branch and the *INSS*.

Non-pensioners

As a non-pensioner, you won't be able to claim any benefits under the Spanish national health system, and you will, as previously mentioned, have to make arrangements for private medical insurance before you are able to obtain your *residencia*. You should of course maintain your DSS contributions in order to ensure that you qualify for a UK pension when you reach state retirement age. If you are working in Spain, then you will have to pay Spanish social security payments of approximately 14,000 *pesetas* a month (in 1988) which will then cover you and your family for medical services.

If you are resident in Spain and approaching the normal state retirement age for a UK pension, then you should write and get form E121 (also from the DSS overseas branch) which should then be sent to the provincial directorate of *INSS*.

Limits to the DSS benefits

It's tempting to believe that even though you live in Spain, you can always use the UK as a last resort if you decide to have that major operation that you have been needing for years. However, that may not necessarily be the case. Although you remain eligible for sickness and invalidity benefits when you **return** to the UK (provided your National Insurance contributions are up to date), your entitlement to receive these benefits only lasts as long as you remain 'ordinarily resident', ie while you actually live in the UK.

Even if you continue to pay National Insurance contributions from abroad to ensure your entitlement to the full basic state retirement pension, those contributions don't automatically give you access to free health care if you return to the UK for a visit. If it is an **emergency**, then you are entitled to it free under the National Health Service, but DHSS leaflet SA34 points out that if the treatment is not an emergency,

then you will have pay for it. Yet another reason for
maintaining your private medical insurance.

Medical insurance

You will no doubt be familiar with the concept of private
medical insurance in the UK but you might not be aware
that it is also very popular in Spain. Spaniards are great
believers in private health insurance and there are over 300
companies in Spain offering a wide range of medical
insurance. Most of these are limited to specific provinces
and selected hospitals and even selected doctors so if you wish
to find out more, you will have to make enquiries in your
own local area.

There are, of course, a number of companies in the UK who
will give you medical insurance whilst you are living in Spain.
It could be that you are already in a suitable scheme and it
may be possible for you to extend it to cover your residence
in Spain. If you are not already in the scheme (and even if
you are) it could pay you to shop around because all the
schemes are different in relation to the benefits that they will
provide once you make a move out of the UK.

The choice of which company to go for can only be made by
you in the light of your own personal circumstances but the
following checklist will give you an idea of the sort of things
that you might think about when choosing the insurance
cover that suits you best:

- Will it restrict your travel abroad?
- Will it cover repatriation costs in the event of major illness
  or death?
- Are there any exclusions for particular sports?
- Are there any exclusions for illnesses you have had in the
  past?

- Are there any illnesses that are not covered (eg alcohol abuse)?
- Is there any type of treatment not covered (eg routine dental treatment)?
- Will it cover the cost of prescriptions?
- What level of hospital costs are covered?
- Will it cover nursing costs?
- Will it cover other members of your family?
- Is there an age limit to joining the scheme?
- Is there an age limit to the benefits provided by the scheme?
- Will the costs increase sharply when you reach a certain age?
- Is there a qualification period for membership in order to be able to start claiming benefits?

Old age

The provision of facilities for **active** retirement has been a growing Spanish industry for the last 25 years.
Unfortunately, little has been done for infirm and elderly foreigners because it has been almost impossible for health care professionals from other countries to work in Spain. Consequently, many long-stay residents are packing their bags for the last time and returning home because of their increasing infirmity. For them, Spain has lost its attraction because they will only feel comfortable about growing old back home.

Many of the more elderly retired find it difficult to remain fully integrated with the Spanish way of life and sometimes the problem of communication becomes greater with increasing age. Being able to share a common lifestyle is very important to older people and there is a strong case for the provision of care for elderly Britons by professionals from Britain who fully understand their needs. There are apartments with help on call, private rest homes and homes providing total care but they are few and far between and they can often be expensive for a retired person.

This is not meant to be pessimistic – it's meant to inject a note of realism. Returning to Britain after a long stay abroad can be a difficult experience in itself and like any house move, it is better to make this kind of major decision whilst you are still fit enough to cope with the inevitable hassle that is going to materialise. Returning to Britain in your early 70s might be a wrench; returning to Britain in your early 80s could be a major problem.

Provision for death

When a foreigner dies, his relatives have several choices. The body can be embalmed and transported back to the UK for burial (or it can be cremated and the urn sent home) or burial (or cremation) can be arranged in Spain. The cemeteries in Spain are almost all Catholic but persons of any religion can be buried there.

Crematoria are comparatively rare in Spain (they are usually only found in the larger cities) so the cost of transport to a crematorium may be considerable.

As you might expect, there are a number of formalities to be observed when someone dies and, under the circumstances, it is usually better to leave everything in the hands of the funeral parlour (the *funeraria*). They will take care of all the details, including the medical certificate, whether the deceased is to be sent back to the UK or whether the burial arrangements will take place in Spain.

It is sensible to make the necessary arrangements to have the sum readily accessible when the unhappy event occurs – for most funeral parlours are looking for cash. You may also find that they operate within closely defined 'territorial limits' so you may have no choice of which firm to employ. It may seem an unusual thing to suggest but it may be worth your while making an exploratory visit to a funeral parlour while you and your partner are both in good health to find out what will have to be done when the need arises. As far as the cash is concerned, it might be a good idea to take out an insurance policy in Spain for funeral expenses and then no one has to worry about the costs at this particularly distressing time.

On a rather more practical point, you should note that if you share a joint bank account with someone who dies, it is wise to transfer the funds into another account as soon as you can as Spanish banks sometimes freeze the account for a time when they learn that one signatory has died.

That all sounds rather depressing and so to end on a rather more helpful note, you might consider when you are a resident of Spain, becoming a member of a local HELP Organisation. Members of HELP are mainly foreigners who are willing to assist other foreigners in case of emergency. The organisation in each area is autonomous and self funding and they will almost always come to your aid in case of trouble or sudden illness and provide assistance for you until permanent arrangements can be made. Don't look to them for any permanent commitments – all HELP members are volunteers who want to be free to assist in **emergencies**.

20 Making a Spanish Will

One of the most common problems in financial life in the UK is that so many people don't like making Wills. Quite why this should be so is not immediately obvious because it is basically so simple. One explanation might be that it's tempting fate to make a Will, but the reality is that it's tempting fate **not** to make one.

A Will is quite simply a statement of what **you** want to happen to your belongings when you die. If you don't leave instructions (which is known as dying 'intestate') then the law will have rules on how your property will be divided up amongst your surviving relatives. These rules may mean that your property is distributed in a way that you would most certainly not have approved of had you been alive. Consequently, writing a Will in the UK can save your family a considerable amount of trouble.

It isn't essential to use a solicitor for drawing up a Will but it's strongly advised that you should do so. Although you may have a very clear idea of how you wish your belongings to be divided up after your death, a solicitor will be able to draft your Will in terms that are completely unambiguous and that is the most important thing. Your Will will be approved by law after your death and it's important then that there should be absolutely no misunderstandings at all about what you actually meant.

The position in Spain

The position is exactly the same in Spain. Writing a Spanish Will is just as straightforward and dying without making a Will can cause your family considerable problems. You may have experienced problems grappling with the Spanish legal system when you were buying your property. Consider what problems your family will have if they're trying to sort out problems after your death under circumstances which might make it very difficult for them to come to Spain and sort the problems out in person. Writing a Will can save a tremendous amount of heartache for them and it doesn't take very long.

It is of course possible to incorporate your Spanish assets into your English Will and that will be usually quite satisfactory. However, it will also be a lengthy process to have your Will proved and that in turn will give your family problems. Having an English Will proved in England can take long enough (two years is not unknown) so it can be imagined just how long it will take to have an English Will proved in Spain. If you've gone to the time and care to produce an English Will, it is no great problem to prepare a Spanish Will for what will normally be fairly restricted assets in Spain.

The form of your Will

There are several forms of Will in Spain but the most suitable one for the majority of people is the open Will (the *testamento abierto*). As with an English Will, there's no need to use a lawyer to prepare your Will but it will be advantageous to do so. By discussing with a Spanish lawyer exactly what you wish to happen to your property after your death, he will be able to take careful note of your wishes and advise you generally on how the Will should be expressed to carry out your true intentions under Spanish law.

As with most legal documents in Spain, your Will has to be

prepared by a notary. You can go (with your self-prepared text or with the text drawn up by your lawyer) to the notary together with three witnesses and the notary will put it into the 'official' format, giving you a copy and sending the original to the Registry of Wills in Madrid.

As with many other legal documents that have to be notarised, it is quite possible to have a Will drawn up in England and then to have it officially handled by the Spanish Consulate in the UK. They will then undertake to make sure that the Will is lodged in Madrid.

Drawing up your Will

There are several points to bear in mind when you are thinking of drawing up a Spanish Will. In the first place, (if you are married) a joint Will has no legality in Spain. Consequently, each party to the marriage must make a separate Spanish Will.

Make sure that the lawyer incorporates a clause dealing with the law of 'quick succession'. This is a common clause in English Wills and covers the case where both you and your spouse are, say, involved in a traffic accident. This ensures that if your spouse dies within, say, 30 days of your death, the inheritance is set aside and all your possessions are passed to the next in line to inherit. This then avoids inheritance tax having to be paid twice on the same assets.

If you have a Will in the UK, it is sensible to ensure that the wording in both Wills is such that they don't conflict.

Appointing executors

With a UK Will, it would not be at all unusual for you to appoint a member of your family as executor, ie the person responsible for ensuring that your wishes are carried out. With Spanish assets, and a Spanish Will, this could be an unfair burden and therefore you should appoint a qualified executor. An *abogado* would be a good choice and it is important here to appoint him before your death and name him in your Will. Under these circumstances, the maximum fees he can charge are limited to 5% of the estate. If you name your bank or a non-Spanish speaking solicitor as your executor they will almost certainly have to instruct a Spanish *abogado* after your death and his fees are then an open-ended expense which will be almost impossible to control.

Keep your heirs up-to-date

Make sure your UK solicitor is completely conversant with the contents of your Spanish Will and make sure that he (and your heirs) know where to find a copy of your Will so that they can locate the notary that recorded it. It is also advisable with your Spanish assets to keep an up-to-date account of all your assets in Spain – property, bank accounts, insurance policies etc.

Your heirs should also be advised of the name of your fiscal representative in Spain. Inheritance tax declarations and the payments of taxes in Spain must be made within six months of your death if you die in Spain and within sixteen months if you die abroad. They should also be aware that inheritance tax must be paid before any change in the title can take place. There is nothing to prevent them from making a private sales contract but transfer of title can only take place after the inheritance has been accepted officially and the inheritance tax paid.

In the same way, you should tell your heirs exactly who your executor is so that they can make contact with him in the event of your death to help him administer and distribute the estate. It would be sensible to keep a close eye on the likely level of inheritance tax that's due to be paid and to discuss with your heirs exactly how this money is to be raised if they don't want to sell the property that they are inheriting.

All in all, making a Spanish Will is a sensible precaution to save your heirs any problems when you die. It's an entirely sensible aspect of financial planning and one which should be undertaken without any delay if you have purchased assets in Spain. It's also advisable to prepare a Will in the UK and you should always keep your Wills up-to-date and reviewed regularly to take account of your changing financial and domestic circumstances.

Appendices

How to appoint a fiscal representative (English and Spanish)

Below is a prototype letter to send to your local delegation of the Ministry of Finances (*Delegación Provincial de Ministerio de Hacienda*). You will find the address in the phone book.

Please note that the person or company appointed must sign the last part of the letter to witness that the representation has been accepted. By signing this form, the person or company appointed accepts the responsibility for ensuring that all your tax liabilities are met. You may therefore be asked to restrict this responsibility to certain types of taxes eg the annual income and wealth taxes only.

'Delegado de Hacienda de . . . . . . (1)

'Ilmo Sr.

Don . . . . . . (2), mayor de edad, con DNI no . . . . . . (3) domiciliado en . . . . . . (4), a VI como mejor proceda, dice:

Que el suscrito es sujeto pasivo para todos los impuestos relacionado con su propiedad en España . . . . . (5).

Que por tanto, viene obligado a designar persona, con domicilio en España, para que le represente ante la Administración Tributaria.

Que la actividad que obliga a dicha tributación se halla situada en su mayor parte, en la provincia . . . . . . (6), por lo que procede presentar la declaración en esa Delegación de Hacienda.

Que se designa como representante a Don . . . . . . (7), mayor de edad, con DNI no . . . . . . (8), y domiciliado en . . . . . . (9) el cual firma este escrito con el firmante en prueba de aceptación expresa.

En su virtud, a VI
SUPLICA: Tenga por presentado este escrito y por designado como representante en España de instante a Don . . . . . . (10) a los efectos prevenidos en el articulo 46 de la Ley General Tributaria.

(Your Signature)   (Signature of representative)

To the Local Delegation of the Minister of Finance for the Province of
. . . . . (1)

Dear Sir,

Mr . . . . . (2), who is of age, with passport number . . . . . (3) living at
. . . . (4), declares:

The undersigned is responsible for all the taxes related to his property
in Spain at . . . . . (5).

For this reason, he is obliged to appoint a person resident in Spain to
represent him before the fiscal administration.

The activity that causes the taxes arises in the Province of . . . . . (6),
which is why the declaration is being sent to this Delegation of the
Ministry of Finance.

He appoints at his fiscal representative, Mr . . . . . (7), who is of age,
with passport number . . . . . (8) and living at . . . . . (9), who has
signed this letter together with the undersigned as proof of his
acceptance.

This letter has been presented and Mr . . . . . (9) has been appointed as
fiscal representative in Spain under all circumstances as foreseen in article
46 of the General Fiscal Law.

(Your signature)   (Signature of Representative)

Key
1 = Province, 2 = Your name, 3 = Your passport number, 4 = Your
address in Spain, 5 = Your property, 6 = Province, 7 = Name of Your
Representative, 8 = His passport/ID number, 9 = His address, 10 = Name
of your representative.

Notification of intent to let (English and Spanish)

If all, or a substantial part of an apartment block is available for letting by a management service on a continuing basis it is classed 'apartamentos turísticos' and must be registered as such with the tourist authorities.

Individual owners who let their apartments, either through a rental agency or privately, are in some Provinces required to notify the fact to the Provincial Tourist Authorities.

Below is a form of words which will help you to do so.

Iltmo. Sr. Jefe de los Servicios Territoriales de Turismo

D. ....
con domicilio fijo en ....
y eventualmente ....
teléfono . . . . . en cumplimiento de los dispuesto en el Real Decreto
2877/82 de 15 Octubre 1982 (BOE 9 Noviembre 1982), presenta la siguiente

Declara que proyecta ofrecer en régimen de alquiler por motivo vacacional o turístico, la siguiente vivienda de su propiedad:

Unidad aislada (apartamento, bungalow, villa, chalet, etc) ....
....
Dirección ....
Teléfono ....
Capacidad de plazas ....
Conforme al Art. 20 de la citada disposición, esta notificación no presume que la Administración garantizo el tipo y calidad de los servicios prestados al usuario, sino que únicamente conceda al declarante la facultad de poder contratar o explotar el alojamiento a que se refiere, sin perjuicio de la competencia de otros Organismos,

. . . . . de 198

DILIGENCIA: Para hacer constar que esta notificación ha sido presentada en los Servicios Territoriales de Turismo en al Provincia.

To the Head of the Territorial Services of the Ministry of Tourism

Mr . . . . . with permanent address . . . . . . and also living at . . . . . (telephone number . . . .), in accordance with the rules established in the royal decree 2877/82 of 15 October 1982 (BOE 9 November 1982), presents the following:

He declares that he intends to let for holidays or short lets, the following property that he owns:

. . . .

address . . . .

telephone number . . . . . .

number of beds . . . .

According to article 20 in the aforementioned rules, this notification does not mean that the administration guarantees the type or quality of the services offered to the user, as it only gives the owner the facility to contract out or use the dwelling, and does not infringe the rights of other areas of the administration.

Dated the . . . . day of . . . . . . 19 . . . .

This is to certify that this notification has been presented to the Territorial Services of the Ministry of Tourism.

Proposal for 'testamento abierto' – open Will (Spanish translation)

En Benidorm, a . . . de. . . . . . ., 19 . . . .
Ante mi, ... Notario del Ilustre Colegio de . . . ., y ante los testigos
de esta vecindad, D. . . . ., D. . . . . y D. . . . ., con capacidad,
siendo los tres mayores de edad, como manifiestan.

– COMPARECEN –

D/Dña . . . ., mayor de edad, casado/a, (profesión), con nacionalidad
. . . ., vecino de . . . ., con pasaporte número . . . .
Manifiesta su voluntad de otorgar testamento abierto: tiene, a mi juicio y al de
los testigos, quienes ven, oyen y entienden y aseguran conocerlo/la, la suficiente
capacidad legal para testar, y manifiesta:
Que es natural de . . . . donde nació el . . . . de. . . . . . . del año
. . . ., siendo hijo/hija de D. y Dña. . . . . (con o sin cualquier otros
antepasados); habiendo contraido primer (segundo) matrimonio con D./Dña.
. . . . (fecha nacimiento), de cuyo matrimonio tienen. . . . . . . hijos llamados
. . . ., y que desea que su ejecución testamentaria sea hecha conforme a la
legislación de su país de origen lo que se consigna en lo siguiente.

– CLAUSULAS –

PRIMERA. – Instituye como único y universal heredero su esposo/a arriba
mencionado/a, D. . . . .
SEGUNDA. – En caso de que el/la esposo/a fallezca antes que el/la testador/a,
instituye como sus herederos, en condiciones iguales, a sus hijos/as arriba
mencionados/as . . . ., sustituyendoles a ellos con sus respectivos
descendientes.
TERCERA. – Nombra Albacea-Contador-Partidor con facultades amplias y con
prorroga del plazo legal, D./Dña . . . ., mayor de edad, vecino/a de
. . . .
Este testamento ha sido otorgado conforme a las instrucciones verbales del
testador/a y encontrandolo de acuerdo con su última voluntad, lo ratifica,
despues de haber sido leido por mi, el Notario, en alta voz, en presencia de
todos, despues de haberles instruido sobre su derecho de leerlo por sí mismos,
del cual renunciaron, y lo firma con los testigos mencionados.

Que yo conozco el/la testador/a y los testigos; que ellos aseguran conocer el/la
testador/a; que la continuidad del acto se ha observado y otras disposiciones
legales; que la capacidad de los testigos, como aseguran, y que todo que se
exprosa en este documento público, yo, el Notario, doy fé. – Está la firma del/
de la testador/a y los testigos. – Firmado y rubricado.

Proposal for 'testamento abierto': open Will (English translation)

In Benidorm the . . . . . of . . . . . of . . . . .
Before me, ..., Notary of the Illustrious College of . . . . ., and before
the three witnesses from this area Mr . . . ., Mr . . . ., and
Mr. . . . . . . who are all of age and able to act in this capacity.

APPEARS

Mr/Mrs . . . ., being of age and married (profession) of . . . .
nationality, resident of . . . . and holder of passport number . . . .

Declares that he/she wishes to execute an Open Will, and has, in my judgment
and in those of the witnesses who listen, see, understand and claim to know
him/her, sufficient legal judgment to do so and who declares:

That he/she was born in . . . . on the . . . . day of . . . . . . 19 ..,
that he/she is the son/daughter of Mr and Mrs . . . . (with or without any
other predecessors); that he/she has been married once to Mrs/Mr . . . .
(born on the . . . . . . of 19   ..) having from their marriage . . . .
children named . . . . . . and that he/she wishes that this testamentary
disposition should conform to the legislation of his/her country of origin as
follows:

CLAUSES

First – He/she appoints his/her aforementioned wife/husband . . . . as sole
beneficiary.

Second – Should the aforementioned wife/husband . . . . predecease the
testator, or in the case of the death of both of them at the same time, he/she
appoints as beneficiaries in equal terms, the aforesaid child/children . . . .
or their respective descendants.

Third – He/she appoints Mr/Mrs . . . . . . being of age and resident of
. . . . as executor with full powers within the meaning of the law.

This Will has been drawn up in accordance with the verbal instructions of the
testator and finding it in accordance with his/her latest wishes, he/she ratifies
it after it has been read aloud by me, the Notary, in the presence of everybody,
(having been instructed of their right to read it themselves which they did not
use) and has signed it with the aforementioned witnesses.

I, the Notary, attest that I know the testator and witnesses and that the witnesses
claim to know the testator and that everything has been done according to law
and that the witnesses are acting with full capacity and that everything expressed
in this public document is correct.

Signature of the testator

Signature of the witnesses

Signed and sealed.

Letter appointing someone to act as your proxy in a community meeting

'Yo, John Smith, propietario del terreno no 3 en la urbanización Bellavista Marbella/Malaga, autorizo a la Sra. Emma Winter, como mi representante para la reunión de la Comunidad de Propietarios que tendra lugar el dia 3 marzo de 1988 a las 10 horas en el Restaurante Cuatro Caminos en la misma urbanización, teniendo mi voto en dicha reunión y todo lo relacionado con ella. Firma y fecha.'

Letter appointing someone to act as your proxy in a community meeting (English translation)

'I, John Smith, owner of the plot no 3 in the urbanisation Bellavista Marbella/Malaga, hereby appoint Emma Winter as my proxy to attend the general meeting of the Community of Owners to be held at 10 o'clock on the 3 of March 1988 in the restaurant Cuatro Caminos in the same urbanisation, or at any adjournment thereof and to vote my shares. Signed and dated.'

It is not necessary to declare a proxy in front of a notary but it must be in writing. If the statutes of the community require the proxy to be declared in Spanish as well the appropriate text is on the opposite page.

Understanding your electricity bill

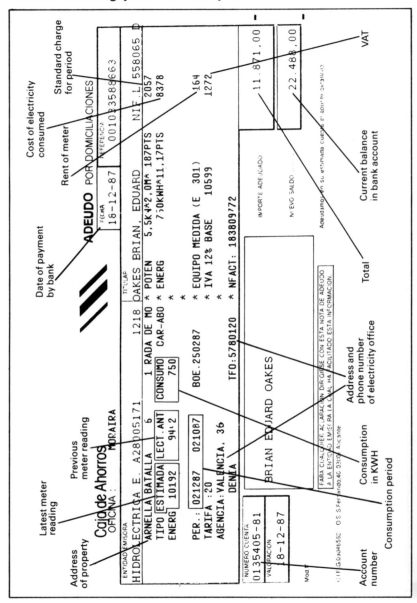

Understanding your water bill

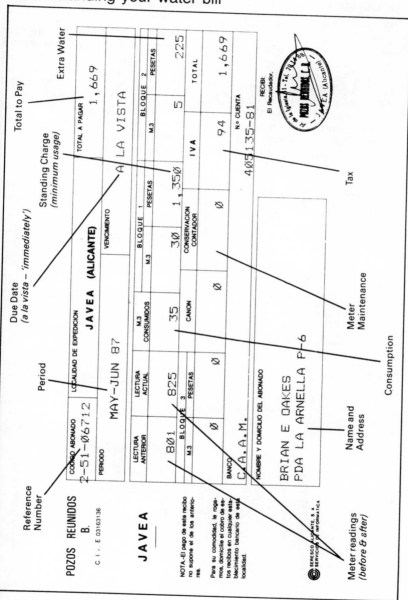

Understanding your rates bill

Ejercicio: Fiscal year. **Delegación:** Delegation. **Municipio:** Municipality. **Zona, Ref. Lista Núm. Recibo:** Internal file information. **Período:** Period covered. **Apellidos y nombre o denominación social:** Name of owner. **D.N.I. o CI:** Identification card or passport number. **Fecha de alta:** Date on which the last assessment was made. **Domicilio Tributario:** Fiscal address. **1-A:** Address of property. **Fecha caducidad, Exención/Bonif:** Expiration date for eventual discount on or exemption from tax. **1-B:** Staircase, floor and door. **2-B:** Land register identificiation number. **3-B:** Basic taxable amount (70% of income value). **% Bonif.:** % discount. **4-B** Net taxable amount. **5-B Catastral:** Official value. **5-B en Renta:** Rental value, 4% of official value.

Cuota: Tax to be paid, 20% of the amount in 4-B. The next two sections are for possible extra charges. **Total a ingesar:** Final amount to be paid.

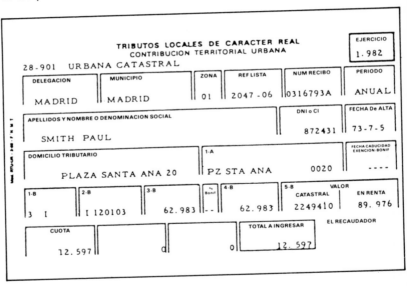

Understanding your bank statement

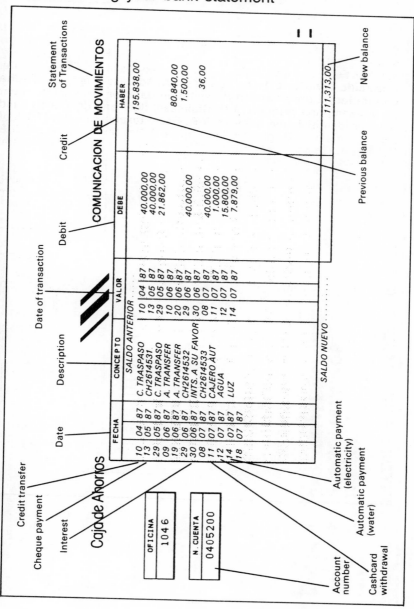

APPLICATION FORM FOR MEMBERSHIP

INSTITUTO
de PROPIETARIOS
EXTRANJEROS, S.A.

U.K. Office: 38 Hillfield Road
West Hampstead
London NW6 1PZ
England
Tel: 01–431 2499
Fax: 01–431 2467

Please enrol me/us as a member/s of the Instituto de Propietarios Extranjeros.

I/We understand that the total membership fee for the first year is £39.00 (incl. VAT) made up of £4.50 enrolment fee plus £34.50 annual fee.

Signature(s) ....

Date ....

	OFFICE USE ONLY		
B	B.I.	Proc/date	Posted

Membership No...................

Institute of Foreign Property Owners
(Block Letters)

NAME (Mr./Mrs./Miss/Ms)..........................

ADDRESS ....

.... County.   Post Code.

Municipality of Spanish Property (if any) ....

Membership by Phone. Call London 01–431 2499 day or night. Quote either Barclaycard, Trustcard or any other VISA or Access account number, name, address and telephone number.

Please debit my VISA or Access card account no.

□□□□□□□□□□□

□□□□□□□□□□□

the grand total of £ ....

Signature ....

OR: I enclose a cheque/postal order for £ ....

Cheques/postal orders should be crossed and made payable to:

Instituto de Propietarios Extranjeros S.A.

Index

Other titles in this series

Managing Your Finances	Helen Pridham
Planning Your Pension	Tony Reardon
Buying Your Home	Richard Newell
Running Your Own Business	David Williams
Tax for the Self-Employed	David Williams
Your Home in Portugal	Rosemary de Rougemont
Planning School and College Fees	Danby Bloch & Amanda Pardoe
Investing in Shares	Hugh Pym & Nick Kochan
Insurance: Are You Covered?	Mihir Bose
Leaving Your Money Wisely	Tony Foreman

Forthcoming titles include:

Financial Planning for the Over 50's	Robert Leach
Your Home in France	Henry Dyson
Your Home in Italy	
Tax and Finance for Women	Helen Pridham